THE REDEMPTIVE LIFE OF A CAYMANIAN WOMAN

THE REDEMPTIVE LIFE OF A CAYMANIAN WOMAN

"Heal me, O' Lord, and I will be healed;
save me and I will be saved, for you are
the one I praise."
Jeremiah 17:14

Sherene Lopez Monzon

Cherish
EDITIONS

First published in Great Britain 2022 by Cherish Editions
Cherish Editions is a trading style of Shaw Callaghan Ltd &
Shaw Callaghan 23 USA, INC.
The Foundation Centre
Navigation House, 48 Millgate, Newark
Nottinghamshire NG24 4TS UK
www.triggerhub.org
Text Copyright © 2022 Sherene Lopez Monzon

British Library Cataloguing in Publication Data
A CIP catalogue record for this book is available upon request
from the British Library
ISBN: 978-1-913615-78-9

This book is also available in the following eBook formats:
ePUB: 978-1-913615-79-6

Sherene Lopez Monzon has asserted her right under the Copyright,
Design and Patents Act 1988 to be identified as the author of this work
Cover design by More Visual
Typeset by Lapiz Digital Services

ENDORSEMENTS FOR *THE REDEMPTIVE LIFE OF A CAYMANIAN WOMAN*

As a prolific author in Caymanian society, it is my observation that Sherene's work is ground-breaking. She has opened a whole new genre of work that serves to edify and provide hope to the vast numbers of people struggling with these and similar issues. The strength of this work is its clear and unequivocal message that complete healing in such cases lies in the belief that we can all be changed for the better through our relationship with God.

I highly recommend this work as a must-read to everyone, irrespective of their faith.

J.A. Roy Bodden, author, educator and Christ follower

This book can teach us many life lessons; whether it is through the anecdotes relayed, the questions she poses or the poetic musings through which she bares her soul, Monzon gives us food for thought. I encourage you to read this book and search your soul, deal with the issues raised and be better individuals, better friends, better spouses, better family members and better followers of Christ.

Erica Gordon, PhD, Assistant Professor at the University College of the Cayman Islands

This book simply captures the author's life journey and shows that there is indeed hope when life seems hopeless. It will definitely benefit those whose lives have been marred by failure and hopelessness and show that, by God's grace and mercy, they can be redeemed and live out God's purposes in their lives.

Bentley Robinson, prison chaplain, HMP Prisons, Cayman Islands

As I read Sherene's book, I felt very touched. She will transport readers into her past world and truly enable understanding and compassion for those in similar situations. We live in an unforgiving world, but we should be reminded of Jesus's own words in Matthew 6:15: "But if you do not forgive men their sins, Your Father will not forgive your sins."

Cathy Gomez, author and former prison chaplain

Here's a testimonial from someone who has thankfully returned from a "far country," while many others have sadly given up hope of ever making it out of such a place. May the unvarnished lessons she has learned inspire many to hope again, and to begin the journey home to the Lord.

Dr. Steve Brady, First Baptist Church of Grand Cayman

For my children Ashley and Matthew Crowe,
my nieces and nephews, and
my parents Vernel and Stanley Clarke of
George Town, Grand Cayman,
Cayman Islands

CONTENTS

FOREWORD

We go through life unaware that, as human beings, we always operate in one or more of the following categories:

1. Pupil
2. Patient
3. Follower
4. Leader
5. Servant

Imagine that all your life, you have been nothing but a pupil, always learning but never achieving; a patient, taking drugs and receiving medical help but never feeling healed or satisfied; a follower, doing something to please your friends even if you believed it was wrong; a leader, always wanting to give instructions; or finally, a servant willing to serve.

Have you ever asked yourself which of these categories you fit into? Perhaps you started by being in one role and then slipped into another? Pause and think, as these categories tell your story! You never want to operate in a category without gaining any perspective. There are some folks who gain perspective, and there are others who die without it.

If you see yourself in one of the above categories and wish to know how you can be delivered, then don't stop reading.

"God, grant me the serenity to accept the things
I cannot change, courage to change the things
I can and wisdom to know the difference".
– Reinhold Niebuhr

DEAR MAMA

Help me this day
to be the daughter you taught to obey.
You've taught me life's lessons, help me not to stray!
I've grown a big woman with children of my own,
I've learned a lot from you, all too soon!
I'm in a condition, not by myself,
and others think they know me so well!
It's only by God's grace that I embrace,
life's journeys, that are so misplaced.
I thank you for all the lessons that I've learned,
although I feel so worn and burned!
Lord, help me take each day at a time
when life's complications are more than a dime.
God created in me a spirit of free will
and taught me further to lean on Him still.
Mama, thank you for all the stories you've shared,
and I'm sorry for all the pain you've carried.
One journey at a time, step by step,
you've shaped my world – that I cannot forget!
God gave you tools to raise a daughter!
What you didn't understand, made you falter.
He's leading me back to instruction,
not to further destruction!
So, I thank Him every day!
With Him leading me,
I know I will find my way.

God bless you, Mama!

THE EARLY YEARS

CHAPTER 1

GROWING UP

At 8lbs, I was a happy and bubbly baby, born at the George Town Hospital and delivered by Matron, the midwife. In those days, doctors did not deliver babies – midwives did. Mama was overjoyed, as I was her second baby girl, and so was my daddy.

By the time I reached the tender age of five years old, I had an acute awareness of God in my life. I could recall frequently praying for world peace. Although I do not recall knowing anything about other countries, I just knew all was not well in my world, as I had heard many biblical stories. Like most children in those days, I played with butterflies and caught bees in little jars. I was so aware of nature and my surroundings.

Many days I found my mama reading a black bonded book, which she hid under her pillow. I was always curious about what was in that book. Although Mama never accompanied her children to church, she would dress me up in the finest clothes and send me off to Sunday school. I later learned that the black book was a Bible. I listened to Mama talking a lot to herself at times and listened to her singing. I laughed many times because my mama could not carry a tune. I followed Mama around a lot by clinging to her skirt tail. I accompanied her on many outings to visit her relatives and friends.

I am the fourth child, second daughter in a family of seven. Being the middle child was no easy role! I often found myself being a mediator, particularly between my mother and father, who seemed to have a tumultuous relationship at the time. My personality reflects both my mother and father, and that made my life very demanding and rather stressful!

What was unusual in our household was that we lived separately. I lived with my mama and siblings, and my father stayed at his family home, but would spend the nights at our house.

Five of us are whole siblings. I have three brothers, two of whom are half-siblings, including Arthur. We had three cousins living with us. Our mother never failed to make room for two or three more.

At times, growing up was a lot of fun, as the house was usually filled with laughter, quarrels and fussing. Mama made all the meals whilst we did all the chores.

My father was very hardworking and dedicated. He was the sole provider for his entire family and put us in good financial standing. He was introverted and, in many ways, I understood his personality, his loss that could not be expressed to his family and all the sadness that he felt. I believed he felt like an outsider in his own home and that he would have liked to reach out to his children, but could not do so because of his upbringing. He had given a lot – perhaps not moral support or loving moments, nor words of encouragement, but stability. I did not feel for one moment that he didn't love me or my siblings. I knew he did, even if it was not expressed.

"My daddy", as he was called by me and my siblings, was conservative. He never readily disclosed information, and his business was kept private, even from mama.

Our mother was very talented, loving, caring, and would serve anyone she came across. She was vivacious, like me, and loved having a great time! Even though the words "I love you" were not often said, she expressed her love in so many ways. She was dependable and considerate of others. She may not have had an opportunity to get a proper education, but she was very smart and intelligent. Our mama was the only foundation on which the family came together as a whole. However, there was a dark side to this mysterious woman: the power to possess and control. Mama wanted people to respect her no matter what.

Although I was simply loved by both parents, my siblings viewed me as the favourite child, and that was unbearable! I am a jovial being, very outspoken and lovable, but had a miserable childhood. I always wondered where I fitted in. I recall that, during my teenage years, I never had an older sibling around as a leader – my brothers were far too busy being boys – so I felt very much alone. And my younger sister Mara and I didn't get along. So, I never felt close to any of my siblings. I never went out of my way to be "different" from any of them. I was a fair person, in all honesty, and I tried to be as reasonable as possible to make people happy, whatever the circumstances. I felt that it was very important for siblings to get to know and understand each other in such a way that there were no ill feelings, particularly when half-siblings were involved. I never viewed my brothers as half-siblings anyway. I firmly believe in family being very much united and, as a child, I felt there was not much unity in the family.

The ins and outs, the ups and downs of families can be so complicated. If only there was better communication among family members, then animosity and selfishness would not take precedence. When these are replaced by love, a family can be so remarkable! So many wonderful things could be achieved, like overcoming struggles. I wonder why we give room to a chaotic way of life. I further believe that order is met through communication, self-control and discipline and, when meshed together, unity provides stability and growth! I also question why siblings like to boss each other around. Is it because of age, gender or perhaps possessions? I can only conclude that self-expression is great and should not be denied! With a little love and a positive attitude, siblings can be such a joy to be around. Embrace them – these relationships can facilitate wonderful accomplishments! A little help for you and a little for me, as God does the rest.

My childhood was very colourful! I did chores, a lot of the time with Mara. Specifically, I remember folding laundry and sweeping and mopping the floors whilst our mother prepared meals. Mara and I also had to take care of our nephew, who was raised by our mother.

Many nights she and I were up late with him, even though we were very young and had to wake up early to go to school.

When our mother was cooking, we were not allowed to be in the kitchen. Mama was the only cook in the house. My daddy worked but faithfully came home for lunch at noon, and he was served the largest meal. Mama was very ambitious as she helped build the family home, which was situated on one of the main streets, Shedden Road, across from the old Merren's grocery store – we knew it as Miss Leola's shop. Oh, how I loved shopping there! We always counted coins over the countertop and bought Paradise candies, along with other niceties. Mrs. Leola paid a lot of attention to me, as she would allow me to attend to customers.

During my childhood, I was the child who was always chastised. No matter how well I behaved, it was not good enough! From doing my chores to having Mama comb my hair, everything was simply hard, I recall. Our mama was a very strict woman! She had a kind personality, but when it came to parenting, we would basically have to do what we were told without any hang-ups. I was often scolded for chatting back. In photographs from my youth, I am usually frowning because when Mama had to press my hair, I would accidentally get burned by the hot comb!

Growing up in the heart of George Town, the capital city of Grand Cayman, was lovely because my siblings and I were close to everything and could easily walk around, although we had to stay in the yard. We were able to play games like cops and robbers with our neighbours; cricket, baseball, marbles and jump rope, too. Our house was very small but busy. There was only a curtain between rooms, separating the boys from the girls.

I must reiterate that I could see God in my surroundings. I became interested in nature in the simplest ways, like looking at the trees, the way they moved and the way the sun hit them. I used to believe that when I moved, the sun and my shadow were following me. I wonder sometimes how in the world there are people who are atheists. There are many unfathomable things in nature. So, I believed then and I believe now that God is very real!

I often looked to the clouds to see if God was sitting up there watching over me. I wholeheartedly believed He watched over everything! I believed so much in His omnipotence, the fact that He had the power to command everything into being, including me!

Living as a child, I saw God in everything, even in the dirt I played in, as in Genesis 3:19, it says, "He formed man from the dust." I even saw God in the way a butterfly flies freely, signifying to me that God is everywhere.

In the grand scheme of things, I see myself as a child of God, and that is spiritual as well as physical. Spiritual in that I am a Christian, and physically because I am made in His image. And my purpose in life is to glorify God.

Connection with the Creator is seeking the things of Christ and living a life worthy of His calling; in other words, being obedient to His guidance, communicating with God and living a life to please Him. Connection is having a constant prayer line, depending on God to sustain you.

I accepted Christ in my life and knew from an early age that I wanted nothing more than to serve Him. So, I started reading through the Bible. The Bible is my favourite book. In my youth, I used to think that it was very complex and contradictory, and so I drifted from it. However, I decided to seek wise counsel and started attending Bible study. I found that my questions were not unfounded, as there were lots of other people seeking to discover what was meant by this or that in the Bible. The more I learned, the more fascinated I became. To this day, I worship the Lord and attend church on a regular basis.

I recall singing songs like "The B-I-B-L-E" and "Jesus Loves Me, This I Know." When it rained and I looked to the sky, I thought the rain must be coming from somewhere, and that somewhere, I concluded, was Heaven, where God sits on His throne.

Proverbs 22:6 says, "Train a child in the way he should go, and when he grows old, he will not depart from it." This is so profound, and although Mama never took us to church, I believed and was sent off to church each Sunday. So, parents ought to give their children instructions on how to live this thing called life. It does not mean that trouble will not come – it will – but one would certainly know how to deal with that trouble much better. God never leaves us or forsakes us. He is always a constant in our lives. It is we who simply remove ourselves from His presence. When we draw near to Him, He draws near to us and can help us whether we are in the proverbial valley or on the mountaintop.

No one told me that God existed. I knew He existed, and I believe that God places that knowledge in each of us, even as children.

As a child, I felt that I was controlled by something greater than myself. I knew that my knowledge was limited and that someone knew a lot more than I did, even more than my parents did, too.

So, where was this knowledge coming from? It could have only come from God, as He created everything in the universe. He is the reason we breathe and live, and then there is death. No human being can dictate these things.

Without God in my life today, I would be void of contentment, that inexpressible joy and the peace that passes all understanding, as described in Philippians 4:6-7: "Do not be anxious about anything, but in every situation, by prayer and petition, with thanksgiving, present your requests to God. And the peace of God, which transcends all understanding, will guard your hearts and your minds in Christ Jesus."

I believe happiness is short-lived, as you can have bursts of happiness. However, contentment and joy are deep-rooted. It is something you experience even when you are going through difficulties and problems. Once you experience peace, you can carry this through any situation. You can even experience that peace amid death if you are assured that it is an avenue to live more abundantly after dying in Christ.

The God of this universe is bigger than our parents. As children, we enjoy all the comforts that our parents can and will offer us. Imagine having abundantly more than that, more than we could ever ask or hope for. Eternal life is promised to all those who repent and believe that Christ died, was buried and rose to life to save us from our sins.

Accepting Him in our lives and living for Him according to His purpose and for His glory brings peace and satisfaction. Human beings cannot and will not be able to sustain themselves – only God can, and He will once we surrender all to Him.

God placed in each one of us a heart, soul and mind to function. With our hearts, we love or hate; with our soul, we feel; and with our minds, we know. So, when we love with our hearts, we can express this love with our feelings and know in our minds that everything we are experiencing is good because it feels right. However, when we hate, it does not have the same effect – we are conjuring evil thoughts and actions, after all. God has placed good and bad in our psyche. When we experience good things, our brains are releasing endorphins, which are feel-good indicators letting us know we are doing something good. When we experience bad things, we do not feel so good. God has given us each the ability to know right from wrong. Our consciousness makes us aware of these good or bad indicators. We know when we are doing something good versus something bad as God, in His Word, has plainly made all things known to us. Romans 18, 19 says, "The wrath of God is being revealed from Heaven against all the godlessness and wickedness of people, who suppress the truth by their wickedness since what may be known about God is plain to them because God has made it plain to them." As Christians, we can spiritually discern, but the man without the Spirit of God cannot discern such things, as stated in 1 Corinthians 2:14.

I do not for one minute believe that I am self-sufficient. Only God is! When one relies on themself, they can become self-destructive. You will discover later how self-reliance played out for me. Self-reliance is contrary to God's dependence. When one relies on themself, we are excluding God.

God is all-powerful, all-knowing and is everywhere. I want to experience this God and to live for Him.

Questions:

1. Have you ever wondered about God?
2. Where do you fit in the grand scheme of things?
3. Do you have spiritual connectedness with the Creator?
4. When was the first time you had an acute awareness of God?
5. Who told you that God exists?
6. Do you have Him in your life now?
7. Would you like to experience the God of the universe?
8. What do you believe about the greater good that lives within each of us?
9. Do you believe you are self-sufficient?

GOD'S AND MAN'S OUTER WORLD

The expanse of God's world is all-encompassing and without lack. The vastness of His embrace is all-consuming, natural and peaceful. His world cradles us like a mother protecting her new-born.

Man's world is fraught with obscure distortions, and desire is like a ship desperately seeking shallow waters. This outer world clashes with God's rhythmic cycle like a dancer not cleaving to a lover. Imagine the shock, the disaster and the desperation to be balancing, holding on, but suddenly falling amid a fused rhythm. It is so typical of humankind's defect by default.

Oh God, help us slip into your world that only a few have a glimpse of. Imagine the night breeze, the cool wind on your face, the stars, the sound of the sea beckoning God's presence, a presence that diminishes the pain, heartaches and deficiency of humankind's nothingness. It is such a comfort to be in tune with a reality few men can fathom.

The two worlds are separate but sufficient, in that one world prepares us for a journey into the spiritual realm, and the other into a well of perdition like a noose seeking to drag us down. The journey is like the flight of a small plane, swiftly cruising although hitting some light turbulence. We feel the movement that gently massages the soul, like that of a child on a joy ride.

The symphony of God's world is forever playing, while the edge of man's outer world has a clear end point. God's world is infinite. Man's outer world is temporal. God's world is cruising along, a vessel seeking to bring us home. Man's outer world can't promise us eternity.

CHAPTER 2

A PUPIL

GRADE SCHOOL

I attended the George Town Primary School, where I settled and met many friends. Every day my siblings and I walked to school, as our house was not too far away. Our lunch was tucked into a brown paper bag and shared by five of us. Walks to and from school were exciting times, as they gave us the opportunity to talk and even buy snacks on the way.

Most of my teachers were from Barbados. In the 1970s, Barbadians were plentiful in Cayman. One of my favourite teachers was Mr. Knight, who wore glasses and was very tall. Mr. Knight was a remarkable teacher, and his penmanship was beautiful! I developed great penmanship from him. Oh, how I enjoyed grade school – it was the perfect escape from the long list of chores I had to do at home. I loved sports and participated in the long jump, high jump and shot put, as well as hurdles. I especially enjoyed Mr. Knight's classes. I was in class 6A, where we learned at a higher level than other pupils. As such, the children in my class did very well and were quick and eager to learn. Mr. Knight always encouraged me with my studies, as he knew I had great potential.

There were other teachers who made an impression on me, including Mrs. Roberts, Mrs. Brewster and Mr. Melano McCoy. I loved going to Mr. McCoy's music lessons as I learned my favourite Christmas carol, "Once in Royal David's City," which remains my favourite to this very day. He was so animated when he conducted the choir.

I learned and absorbed things quickly as I am a visual learner. Even today, if I see something, I can often easily imitate it. I was sharp on my feet and always had a great quip ready, much like my mama. I had a knack for making others comfortable.

Back then, pupils were split into tutorial groups named after flowers. They were Zinnias, Shamrock, Hibiscus and Periwinkle. I was in Shamrock. Mrs. Roberts and Mr. Knight were my teachers. I recalled the children teasing Mrs. Roberts with, "Roberts, you want some pop? Look in the big Dutch pot. Whether you like it or not, take off your shoes and hop." This brought a lot of laughs amongst all of us students.

Although Mama did not have much, she made certain she had a few parties for Arthur and me. Arthur was usually the life of the party with his infamous dance moves, much like a karate kid. My mama would invite lots of children from the neighbourhood. When we had parties, we did not eat off paper plates, but rather out of paper napkins and cups. All the food would be smashed together – cake, chips, corn beef sandwiches – and yet, they were still tasty. Those really were the good ole days!

I had many friends, both in primary school and later in high school. My friends back then were more like sisters – sometimes we even dressed alike. However, despite the many friends that I had, I was not allowed to sleep over at their houses. My siblings and I always had a curfew.

School life for me at the primary school level was enjoyable, as we got to play a lot and did fun things: netball and other various sports, and we even had dance contests. I recall one of my cousins, Barry, entered a dance competition with me at primary school, and we won the title of "Best Dancers." He and I were so happy.

As mentioned earlier, I had a lot of childhood friends. However, I would often frown because children were told to "speak when you are spoken to, don't chat back, be seen but not heard." I was a very determined and strong-willed child. I wanted to have my way, but Mama knew how not to let me.

RELIGIOUS BACKGROUND

I knew I wanted more than anything to serve God first. I surrendered my life to God, whom I knew for certain would take good care of me. I have seen the work of God in many situations in my life.

As a child, I attended Church of God Universal and later moved to Elmslie Memorial, a united Presbyterian Church on the waterfront. This was the family's church home. There, I was taught about Jesus and was told Bible stories by my Sunday School teacher, Mrs. Helen Merren of George Town, of whom I am quite fond to this very day! A reprieve from being miserable at home, I attended Christian Endeavour, led by the Late Noel Johnson of George Town. I recall walking from the waterfront to South Sound to go to Mrs. Ella's beach and Smith Cove, and I specifically remember the group walking in the dark to get there. Oh, how I loved to attend Sunday School and later church. I used to say, "If I could live in a church, I would be so happy because once you step out, you're in the world of sin." Funny, but it is true because at church everyone behaved "good" and "decent." Outside of church, the world appeared to be filled with misery and problems.

I later attended Girls' Guildry, which focused on Christian fellowship and enhancement of girls' lives through following Christ. Girls' Guildry came to Cayman from the United Kingdom. There were several heads, including the late Mrs. Olive Miller, Mrs. Iva Good, the late Mrs. Elizabeth Hurlston and others who were instrumental in Girls' Guildry in Cayman, now called Girls' Brigade.

There were four phases to Girls' Brigade: Explorers, Juniors, Seniors and Brigadiers.

I favoured the Explorers' entry level, as Mrs. Effie Johnson and Mrs. Emily Seymour taught the little ones. I was quite keen on listening to Mrs. Effie's storytelling in character style, which piqued so many of my interests. Mrs. Effie was very kind and in later years, I would re-visit Girls' Brigade to assist her and Mrs. Emily with the Explorers. I very much enjoyed arts and crafts and helping each child, even the ones that misbehaved. As I recall, there was plenty of that going on from some of the children, particularly those from George Town.

I learned to march in a straight, no-nonsense line, particularly with Mrs. Louise watching. She kept a strict eye on me, as I was not favoured by her. Nonetheless, I paid close attention, as she took marching seriously! Later on came Mrs. Ella Kay, Mrs. Harriet Vassell and Mrs. Emily, who was stern too! Boy, they had to keep up with us. However, Girls' Brigade was indeed great discipline and lots of fun.

I enjoyed getting together with all the Brigadiers (young adult ladies) from each district as we would gather for togetherness, sharing and exchanging gifts and talents, even going on retreats to Prospect House! As I recall, they were awesome times. I specifically recall the picnics on the lawn at the Manse on South Church Street, where I met a lady from England, who to this day remains in Cayman. She too taught Brigade and, oh, she was stern and commanding of our attention. She would say, "Oi," as I suspect there were too many names for her to recall.

I, along with many childhood friends, attended faithfully each week and learned many skills including dancing styles – figure of eight, do-si-do and the waltz – as well as how to set a table, which utensils to use for each meal and, of course, how to march.

When I became old enough, my mama would allow me to attend Christian Endeavour, where, along with others, I praised and worshipped the Lord, and we went camping with really huge bonfires! I remember the youth group doing a play on the beach, imitating the passion of Christ long before the movie ever came out. You could see the iron shore and pick up whelks at the Prospect House – this was so much fun. The late Noel Johnson and Thomas "Tally" Myles were in charge back then. Later, Christian Endeavour became Koinonia, which was less fun, as I recall: we took few road trips to the other districts and had no plays or huge bonfires. It could very well be that I had stopped attending.

Although I grew up attending church, I was never fully satisfied, as later in life, I wandered from church to church but had a desire to attend faithfully each week.

Questions:
1. Do you believe in attending church?
2. Is church a necessary part of a Christian's life?
3. Is church membership important?
4. How does church fit into your lifestyle?
5. Do you believe children should attend Sunday School?
6. Do you believe that church should play a part in your children's life?
7. Do you believe in church youth groups?
8. Would you send your young adults to church camps?

ADULTHOOD

CHAPTER 3

A PATIENT AND A FOLLOWER

I was often told that I was the apple of my father's eye! However, looking back, I realize this caused a big rift between my father and mother. I believe that my mother treated me so harshly because I was my father's favourite, too. Nevertheless, my mother and other siblings helped raise me.

Ideally, it is great to have both parents in a household to nurture and raise children. However, it was not the case in this family, but my mother did an exemplary job raising her seven children plus those she took in.

HIGH SCHOOL

At the age of 11, I attended the Cayman Islands High School, where subjects were chosen, unlike in primary school, where everything was taught together. I mostly chose business subjects: commerce, office practice and typewriting. Another teacher I remember from high school was Miss Chambers, later called Mrs. Shacklady. Oh, how my friends and I teased this teacher... we were very mischievous!

Spanish was taught at the high school level, and it was because of my teacher's attitude in this class that I succumbed to a nervous breakdown. The reason was that my Spanish teacher Miss Daniels was quite miserable, and she brought it to school! Could it be that she was having issues herself? Sometimes, she was unbearable!

I remember the day I was put out of the class. I tried to pay attention but kept interrupting for lack of understanding. So, I was removed from the class and placed in the principal's office.

Mr. Whiteside, who was firm yet loving to me, let me sit and do my work peacefully. I suffered a nervous breakdown during this critical period in my life. I was taken overseas to St. Joseph's Hospital in Jamaica. My parents took me to a psychiatrist and reverend named Joseph C. Cook for treatment, as they could not figure out my behaviour, particularly backchatting.

Although I did not know it at the time, my mother must have been called in to school to talk about my behaviour. As reiterated, Mama was no-nonsense and headstrong, but I believed my mama queried why I was not in class. Most children who were presumed difficult to handle were sent off to Jamaica.

When we arrived at the hospital in Jamaica, my parents and I were ushered into an office. There sat a tall, elderly man, the psychiatrist, Reverend Joseph C. Cook. He had kindness in his eyes! Mama explained why we were there as my father sat quietly. Then, discussions were held between Mama and Reverend Cook before my parents left the room so that he and I were left to chat. My parents were called back in, and the reverend finally said, "Nothing is wrong with this child. She is just going through an adolescent crisis!" I now realize this meant that I was going through puberty, transitioning from childhood to adulthood.

At the time, I didn't understand what was happening, but I went away feeling good, as the reverend concurred that nothing was wrong with me. However, that was never good enough for my mama. Perhaps she was learning something too!

I presumed my parents and I were going back home to the Cayman Islands, only to end up on the psychiatric ward at St. Joseph's for a short period of time. Whilst there, I met a very unkind nurse. When I was attended to, I was stabbed with injections to silence me. Mama was unaware of this, as she was taken away during this treatment.

However, just sending me to a psychiatrist was apparently not good enough, particularly for my mother, who could not stand my backchatting. Of all the siblings, I had a mouth that just had to talk back. I was very loving but stubborn!

As I recall snippets of my childhood, life felt unbearable at times. So began this medical journey, as I was taken from psychiatrist to psychiatrist because of my mother's intolerance.

I firmly believe that children should be guided but also be able to express themselves in such a way that they are not deviating from their true selves. That they should be heard and not be hushed, particularly when they are trying to relay a message. Oftentimes, children are put on medication to control their behaviour rather than getting to the root problems in the child's life. For example, if a child is disruptive or overactive, ask the child questions rather than disciplining the behaviour right away.

In my early teenage years, I was instructed by God to lead a Bible study at my parents' house. However, all of a sudden, I became ill and was taken away to Jamaica again. I was determined to do my own thing. So, in 1984, I went away by myself to the UK. I stayed with the Martins, who I had met in Cayman. I went to their home for one month and told my mama I was not coming back to Cayman. However, I did return.

I was elated with the new changes after my trip, so much so that I again wanted to start my own Bible study. However, it was as if no one wanted me to serve God first. Shockingly, I became ill again. In periods when I became ill, God drew me back to Himself, signifying that He is indeed real! I always felt secure in the knowledge of Him.

Throughout my teenage life, I was determined to serve God. However, I kept on straying from the word, doing my own thing. I loved a good party! I enjoyed dancing and going out with my friends but never gave up on Sunday School.

Nevertheless, I found myself partying and carousing with friends and strangers. I went to a lot of dances, festivities and even hosted parties. I knew how to draw people from different walks of life together. I had leadership qualities, but I appeared many times as a follower, doing what others expected of me rather than what was best. I pleased others well!

From time to time, my illness had me drained as I tried keeping up with everything. Little did my family and friends know that I had to try very hard to simply be myself, the way God created me to be.

Throughout high school, I missed a lot of classes because being on medications would keep me away from school. It was so difficult as I struggled to stay abreast of my studies and keep up with friends.

I graduated in 1984 and later attended the community college, where I continued in business studies, together with English for business communication. In 1992, I passed the entrance examination to attend the International College of the Cayman Islands, where I further studied. Due to my circumstances, I was unable to complete my studies there. My father, although he barely helped with schoolwork, wanted me to be a lawyer!

In early times at the Law Offices of Radcliff and Dover, I was the apple of the attorneys' eyes, as I made them laugh and was interested in each of their lives. Sometimes, if an attorney or perhaps a secretary, janitor or visitor in the elevator would not say good morning or even offer a greeting, I would say to them, "Good morning, did I sleep with you last night?" This joke brought beaming smiles to their faces. Later in life, at family discussions, my little sister Polly – big sister in mind – would say, "[The people in the elevators] had no manners." Others mistook it for prejudice. However, when discussions such as those came up, I retorted, "It could be that they were preoccupied." Although prejudices exist, it is nonsensical to be that way, as God created each one of us to be uniquely different. I chose to ignore any negative comments.

In spite of my outgoing nature, throughout my high school life and after periods of illness, I simply had to start all over to learn how to do simple tasks and overcome many obstacles. It was not an easy journey. There were numerous times that I cowered at family gatherings. I could not keep up with conversations. During those periods, everything simply went over my head. To this very day, I must try very hard to retain information. However, God never, ever gave up on me! He led me all the way to this point of writing my own book, poems, autobiography and even prepared me to write two more books!

Following others was never my desire, as I was comfortable being who I am even before illness tried taking control of my life through external forces.

However, I was determined to stick it out to the very end. Although I did not complete a bachelor's degree programme, I was finally getting somewhere later in life as I earned my paralegal diploma, receiving the highest honour. My teacher Mr. Anthony White was delighted to have taught me in this course.

I desired to study further; however, it did not happen as circumstances did not permit it.

Questions:
1. How was your childhood?
2. Did both parents raise you?
3. Did you have many friends?
4. How was your school life?
5. Were you a late bloomer?
6. How were you in a social setting?
7. Did you have any profound illness as a child? How did it affect you?

CHAPTER 4

EMPLOYMENT

I was vivacious and was the life of the party! I worked in one of
the most prestigious firms in the Cayman Islands. I was punctual,
loyal and hardworking! All the attorneys admired me for my lively,
spirited nature and my straightforwardness. I commanded much
attention, and it was freely given to me. I made everyone I came
across feel comfortable and at home. Whether they came from other
places or the Island, they were happy to have met me. Even the
most serious and timid attorneys laughed heartily around me.

The firm at which I worked was very structured in that the
staff who worked for the attorneys were rotated every six months.
From litigation to corporate to conveyancing, to commercial law,
patents and trademarks, everyone had a chance to experience the
different areas of practice. I most enjoyed my time in the litigation
department, where I met a lovely attorney! This attorney swept
me off my feet, as I just loved his accent. Every so often, ladies
and gents would gather around my desk as I ordered lingerie from
Victoria's Secret and Frederick's of Hollywood! The parties that
were periodically held were a lot of fun, too, and everyone looked
forward to them. From boat trips to lip-syncing and Christmas
funnies, we always had a good laugh. One of my tricks was pulling
pranks on the attorneys and using caricatures to display their sullen
behaviour. One time at another firm, the staff was awestruck when
I sat on the managing director's lap to get him out of his shell.
This brought many laughs and broke the ice, as I was at a staff
Christmas lunch.

I delighted in introducing foreigners to my mama's house. People came from far and near to have a taste of Mama's cooking! I was no stranger to talking, as I expressed myself candidly. I brought different races, nationalities and ethnic groups together. Back then, I was a great conversationalist, and I was not afraid to blend! My friends admired me, and some were envious too. I encouraged them and I was the friend who could always be counted on.

CHALLENGES AND BEYOND

CHAPTER 5

BIPOLAR

I was formally diagnosed with bipolar affective disorder, referred to simply as bipolar, in 1992 by Dr. Fawn of Jamaica. Bipolar is commonly known as manic depression, which encompasses high-to-low mood swings. Mania is said to be when someone exhibits God-like behaviours, or an over-abundance of confidence; of course, I largely disagree with this description.

Depression is the opposite of mania: low feelings, low self-esteem, feelings associated with experiencing death or grief. However, the prognosis for those with bipolar affective disorder can be exaggerated and misleading; every patient's case will be different, and those unfamiliar with the condition need to realize that.

I believed that anyone with a bipolar condition would only find it worsened by some forms of psychiatric intervention, whether practiced in America or any other country in the world. I saw it as a priority that people everywhere should seek freedom through God in order to save themselves from evil corruption. More and more, the world is evolving, and yet there is still stigma surrounding bipolar and many other diseases, thereby creating disorder and confusion. We must turn back to God's plan for civilization. Even the animals are depleted and cannot readily find food because of the planet's lack, which is down to humankind's greed.

However, in my opinion and in my personal experience, being some 30-odd years old, a female, mother of two, middle child and a very independent, strong-willed individual, it has been quite a phenomenal experience, exploring various aspects of the illness known as bipolar.

Of course, not everything everyone hears about this disease is accurate; what is heard can be largely exaggerated and exploited. All of us suffer from mental illness at varying degrees, but not everyone operates the same. However, it was and is common to lump everyone with the same diagnosis in the same basket, which can be even more detrimental to one's state of mind.

I believe that we are all unique – in some cases similar but not altogether the same. Therefore, mental illness should be discussed and treated on a case-by-case basis that is aligned to the patient's makeup mechanism.

It is important to have family, friends and the general community involved in the treatment process, bearing in mind that they won't always be in consensus – they will have to learn to agree to disagree. However, the patient ultimately knows quite a lot and is often the most useful source of information, if given the opportunity to so explore. In other words, cues should be taken from the patient to facilitate treatment and help the doctor, family, friends and the community. Everyone in the process, essentially, will achieve their optimal results.

I could have died many times, but with my belief in God and the willpower that he gave me, I persevered. It's important to tap into your God-given abilities, which provide comfort and healing. God does provide good doctors and people, but there are some who are after their own agenda. God doesn't sleep nor slumber, and in His care, I am ultimately deemed healed and strengthened.

An illness is a part of life and is one of the many aspects that make the world go around. We need each other to get through it: sisters and brothers; mothers and fathers; friends and community. Embrace God's world and reach for the stars!

On 1 October 2010, I wrote that I felt that bipolar affective disorder could be a sort of camouflage for something else that is plaguing our society. I believed that we all have a chemical imbalance of sorts. However, it is an imbalance that occurs physically, spiritually and mentally.

In my view, when we stray from what is essentially good for us, we cannot cope; we are indeed affected because something has broken down. Essentially, we need to find out what it is that caused our dilemma.

We know that, for a period, we are physically strong and well, that everything's okay, and then suddenly, we become sick. Whether it's a simple headache or cold, something is not right. This means that we have been broken in some way, that our bodies are not functioning in the way in which they were designed. We need to seek the cause, as these uncomfortable reactions occur in the chain of causation. We need to recognize first that we are spiritual beings. Secondly, we are made physically. Thirdly, if those parts are in discord, people will break down mentally.

On 1 October 2020, I continued to write:

PHYSICALLY

Those of us who were born without deformity are, by definition, physically fit beings who can enjoy a variety of activities. People can learn and engage in any sport if they are willing. Some of us are not so fortunate because we simply were not born that way, so our strengths, functions and gifts are developed and exercised in other areas.

God gave me a perfect body! As I developed, I watched my body's growth. I have found flaws along the way, but my body was still pleasing to me. However, over the years and periods in my life, I realized my body had changed tremendously even before having children, and it was not maturing in the way that God intended. Specifically, I realized that my body had aged much more rapidly than it was supposed to. At a certain point, it was no longer pleasing to me. I also learned that those changes were caused directly and/or indirectly. Now, at 54 years of age, I've looked back again and discovered that I could have maintained my form if I had lived my life according to God's guidance. However, circumstances and events unfold in one's life that are controlled by other forces, and when you give in, you cannot retain the benefits of living a life that is pleasing to God. Therefore, there are sometimes consequences.

SPIRITUALLY

We were born with intuition and purpose. When we discover at an early age that God is our Creator, we are given instructions on how we must please Him because He first loved us. He is the reason we are on this earth. If we believe, we will have a thirst for this knowledge and will want to exercise this truth! So, we embark on a journey of being the good Samaritan. God's intention for us is to live holily, live in righteousness and obey His commandments. Fundamentally, if we believe this, our intention is to follow through. However, because of human nature, all have sinned and fallen short of God's glory, so we lose ground. By the same token, believers know God's purpose and know what our goal is. If we want to remain in Him, we will continue to strive for that goal. It doesn't matter if we lose ground from time to time, God has His hands on us. It is we who must recognize that if we should detach ourselves spiritually, we will suffer grave consequences and will not live the life that we are called to. Therefore, we must be obedient to God's calling and revert to our goal of being secured in the knowledge of Him and in the assurance that He will deliver us! As He reminds us in His Word, He will never leave us nor forsake us, and He will never fail us once we are obedient to His guidance.

MENTALLY

Should we neglect our physical and spiritual well-being, we will simply have huge problems mentally! When we are broken physically, we are affected mentally, and when we are spiritually disconnected, this makes us unwell too. God wants us to be healthy in all aspects of our lives. However, there are other forces that are dragging us down, but we only need to keep the goal in mind and, no matter what obstacles come our way, God will deliver us. Our struggles, problems, difficulties, disappointments and rejections can be turned into good. If we are secured in the knowledge of Him, we will use negatives as our strengths to push forward to reach our goal. Therefore, you must know what the goal is and what you need to do to get there. It is my desire that you trust God and that you will experience liberty in every area of your life. Even if you have difficulties and are in the valley, God is there to pull you through.

IN CONCLUSION

When we abuse our bodies physically and spiritually, we become broken mentally. This doesn't mean we are sick; it means we need to fix something for the mechanisms to function together as a whole.

INSOMNIA

I also believe one of the exacerbating factors for those with bipolar is sleep deprivation. Sleep is so important! A lack thereof can be crippling in a lot of areas. For example, your cognitive ability may be compromised. When this happens, I am unable to follow a topic for too long. My memory is also affected, as I can't recall or repeat information, even if it was just told to me less than five minutes prior.

Having these difficulties, one must learn how to cope by exercising the mind, whether they do so by reading, keeping active or pursuing their hobbies.

I recall after having children that my sleep drastically declined. I couldn't sleep through the night and, for years, I have been unable to do so. Even though my mind was at peaceful rest, and I did not have thoughts replaying in my mind once I settled into bed, I was generally aware of being awake. I cannot fall asleep in the daytime. Even with a regular sleep time, it is so difficult to fall asleep. However, it is very important that you do rest.

I was diagnosed with sleep apnea and have been given several different types of sleeping devices. However, so far, they have not been helpful to me, as I have tossed and turned more with the devices on than off. It has been a constant battle, but one I'm determined to pursue to improve my health.

CHAPTER 6

MISMANAGEMENT OF MENTAL HEALTH PATIENTS

In Cayman, the mental health law is outdated, especially as I recall the handling of mental health patients. When patients at the George Town hospital presented as unbalanced, they were not attended to by the ER doctors because they were mental health patients; instead, the psychiatrist was called to dole out treatment. At one stage, I was physically ill and not mentally incapacitated. So, instead of dealing with my physical state, I was being treated mentally. This often led to hospitalizations during which I was treated for being mentally ill and given drugs that further affected my psyche, rather than treating the physical state. Drugs were given at such high dosages that they were difficult for the local doctors to manage. In times like these, patients were flown overseas for treatment, as it could not be done in George Town. It was difficult for the local psychiatrist to balance the patient's mental capacity and physical state at the same time. In other words, some were being treated for a mental condition when they needed to be treated physically, which resulted in a mental breakdown and inability to function. This can be very dangerous and detrimental to the patient's well-being.

I required healthcare overseas and, in most cases, I was flown to Cleveland Hospital in Ohio. There, I was cross-examined, and they always took me off all the drugs given by the psychiatrist in Cayman. I was further observed for a few days, re-evaluated, and then new drugs were slowly administered at a manageable, steady dosage. This usually took about two to three weeks of treatment, and then I was discharged to my family. I was usually sanctioned, as I did not readily accept that I had bipolar affective disorder.

Here in Cayman, some psychiatrists prescribe mental health patients' medication at the highest dose and work down to a lower one, rather than starting at the lowest and building up to the highest.

I've also seen how ailments such as an ear infection or cold – common conditions that can throw off a patient's equilibrium – are often seen as mental incapacity. Therefore, it is critical for medical professionals to listen and pay attention to the patient, first and foremost. On top of that, many patients are sent to the inpatient mental health ward for simple conditions that can be treated with outpatient care.

In my experience, a stay once took more than a month. I remember being called a very wise patient as I queried all the drugs given and was also adamant about not taking drugs so readily, based on how they made me feel.

At one stage, the then-psychiatrist referred to me as his "A" student. I felt that my symptoms were also tied to my spiritual self, for I was always reverting to thoughts of the universe and God's creation.

Another mismanagement in Cayman that I found to be extremely cruel was that the law required policemen to take mental health patients into custody even though they did not commit any crime. Policemen often handcuffed and ill-treated the patients. In my case, this scenario played out numerous times.

One time, I was arrested on the ground in front of some family members at my home. My family did not even fend off the policemen, who created a scene of utter brutality. I will never forget such barbaric treatment. When patients are taken into custody, they are jailed or sent to prison for naught. This is cruel and can lead to criminality. I believe that mental health nurses should be trained to handle patients and should themselves be on call to collect those who present as mentally unwell.

Once in custody, misunderstood, loud patients are often injected and put into isolation for speaking out. They receive high doses of medication and then present as being out of their minds – they do not recognize anyone or know how to perform basic functions. These patients are often left for long periods of time in isolation, sometimes without water or bathroom breaks.

Many times, patients are dosed to high levels, and they walk around as if they are mad. This situation can get so bad that patients walk around like zombies, not knowing what is taking place or what they are doing. In some cases, patients eat out of garbage cans and feed off leaves rather than taking their medication, all because of the drugs' adverse effects, which can exacerbate a patient's condition, rather than making it better.

In my case, I was isolated and drugged many times. When I was given an opportunity to go outside, I ate leaves, as I believed them to be cleansing and healing. However difficult my situation became, I had an acute awareness of God, and I firmly believed that I was not "sick". My treatment process was harsh, and treatment for mental health patients in Cayman needs to be investigated and corrected.

Although I believe that a facility is necessary for mental reprieve, I believe that the size of the present facility is sufficient. I do not believe that a larger mental health care facility is necessary, as I imagine it will serve as an excuse to house many people who do not necessarily need to be institutionalized. It is like building a bigger prison: if it's built, more prisoners will be needed to occupy it. It is an unnecessary evil! So, I think that patients need to be treated as needed and released, not institutionalized.

MEDICATION

Each person is different: while some can tolerate one medication, others cannot and will need another option. However, some drugs do carry certain side effects that need to be considered. Haloperidol is one such drug that affects many patients; so is clopixol. Haloperidol was one of the first drugs given to me by one of the earlier psychiatrists who was a resident in Cayman Brac. It is known to treat hallucinations, and yet I do not recall ever seeing things *until* I was given this drug. Plus, if this medication is given at high dosages, it can leave people confused and completely unaware of what they are doing. So, this drug can be detrimental to one's well-being if not used correctly.

Throughout my life's journey, I have taken numerous medications like Depakote, or valproic acid, which is used to treat seizures, but is also administered to people with bipolar disorder. I have never had a seizure in my entire life. This medication had to be monitored closely – my white blood cells had to be checked every month. I could not ingest salt or go out in the sun because of the various effects the drugs had on me. If I was in a manic state and took valproic acid at a higher dose, this made me more manic. I experienced the same side effects if I ate table salt.

When someone takes medications such as mood stabilizers, they must be extremely careful with taking over-the-counter medications and ingesting caffeine at the same time. They may also have to avoid eating certain foods. Simple things like painkillers or cough syrups can be dangerous when taken in tandem with these medications. Do your research. Most times, it is difficult to reach a doctor or get the necessary help at a moment's notice, so you need to be able to help yourself. If you have the necessary tools to do so, this can potentially save your life.

I took numerous prescriptions in the more than 30 years that I was on medication: lithium, Tegretol, risperidone, Ativan (lorazepam), temazepam, clonazepam, Zyprexa (olanzapine), Effexor, Clopixol, Seroquel (quetiapine), lamotrigine and Abilify. Some of the potential side effects of these medications include changes in menstrual cycle, excessive weight gain, blurry vision, memory impairment, confusion and so many others.

I am not saying that these medications are bad; what I am saying is you need to know when and for what you are taking them. Depending on how you react to them, some side effects can feel less than curative. For example, certain epileptic drugs – haloperidol and clopixol – should not have been administered to me because they made me deviate from my normal. My nails grew excessively long, my hair suddenly grew thicker, and facial hair appeared, too. I looked glassy-eyed and felt very strange.

I think there should be required medication education, as so many patients are unfamiliar with or cannot decipher the medications they have to take. For example, when someone gets a new prescription, the psychiatrist should provide a printable summary on the drug. Give the patient specific written dos and don'ts for their medication. If any negative side effects arise, the patient should know to report it to their doctor. Also, the doctor should teach the patient how to manage the drug and whether they can increase or decrease the dose – and how high or how low they can go. This is, of course, specific to the patient's condition and stability and whether the patient can self-manage to a certain degree.

I was always reluctant to take any drug because I felt they compounded or exacerbated my problems. I would generally do my homework after being given the medications. Some doctors did not like that. I also took it upon myself to read pill books about my medication, which I was discouraged from doing. However, I was adamant about understanding and sharing how they made me feel, which I found to be worse than before. I did not give up on querying drugs, as I knew how I felt was important, and it was not God's way to make me feel worse after taking the drugs.

I remember one summer when my kids came home, I could not play with them because I was too fatigued and heavily sedated. This went on for months. However, I did not let it deter me from believing who God created me to be: whole and sound. I also focused a lot on self-control, one of the fruits of the Spirit that kept bringing me through each time I had an episode. You have to be very strong when you are under doctors' care; otherwise, you will not be an active agent in your own recovery.

MENTAL SUICIDE

I believe if you are a mental health patient taking medications, you ought to examine and study the drugs that are prescribed for you. You should also be very aware of the way they make you feel. In my experience of being in a very depressed state, certain medications at the wrong dosage *heightened* my inability to cope. The same can also be said for those in mania – high dosages might tip you further over the edge, as they did for me. I know I am not a doctor; however, I have had enough experience to note this. I also feel that if it was not for my belief in God, I could have died many times.

Medications can help. However, to anyone in a desperate, depressed or manic state, I would recommend seeking a psychotherapist first, then proceeding to a psychiatrist. Many times, I just needed someone to talk to, someone who could meet me at my level, walk me through whatever I was going through at the time, and help me to sleep. I would ask to go on long drives, go to the beach, write, dance, or sing my Christian and secular songs that I enjoyed. Many times, I got through that way. Talking helps in a huge way. Rather than talking ad nauseam to one friend, find a circle of close friends who make themselves available to you. As it is written in Proverbs 15:22, "Plans fail for lack of counsel, but with many advisers, they succeed."

I still take medication; however, I am on a very mild dose and have learned to manage my meds. This did not happen overnight. This happened by being totally honest with my doctor and adamant about things that didn't feel right. I was also sure to ask the doctor questions pertaining to weight, nutrition and exercise, as well as any other illnesses that I had to treat at the same time.

I also firmly believe that women with mental health conditions benefit from having psychiatrists who are women. From my experience and what I have seen with other women, our problems are often linked with hormonal imbalances from the menstrual cycle. We need to be in tune with our bodies and what happens mentally during hormonal shifts, and no one understands that better than other women.

To the feeble of heart, I say, surround yourself with people who are connected spiritually, stronger than you are mentally, fitter than you are physically, and healthier than you are. Should you seek to do this in low times, you will get the necessary help and reassurance to overcome your obstacles. However, do not just stop there; it is a lifelong battle, but God, great Christian friends, connection with your community and the church will help you along your life's journey. So, believe in yourself, and tap into your God-given abilities. He will lead you to people who will genuinely help. Get involved in charitable organizations. Do not sit idly, but find time to engage in activities and enjoy and celebrate life. This may seem difficult when you are depressed, but don't be a recluse and go on your life's journey alone. Reach out, embrace life, and you will see a difference in your thought processes and your attitude, all of which will bring you success in every area of your life, even in difficult times.

> *"I will instruct you and teach you*
> *in the way which you should go;*
> *I will counsel you with My eye upon you.*
> *– Psalm 32:8*

CHAPTER 7

MENTAL HEALTH

In any culture, mental health needs to be acknowledged as part of its society. Mental illness is no different than physical illness – it's a condition that incapacitates our ability to function on a normal or ordinary basis. It is therefore essential that mental illness be treated the same as physical illness in terms of care and attention. Caregivers should give compassionate treatments, as opposed to harshly handling their patients.

In my experience, mental health patients are very loving and caring. The periods where mental health patients would become aggressive coincided with poor handling of their condition or care.

Some psychiatrists contribute to mismanagement of mental health patients because they are so bent on doling out medicine instead of prescribing psychotherapy for the patient, which is often the better method. Medicine is not all bad. However, with mental health patients, strong anti-psychotic drugs can immobilize or incapacitate someone or limit their ability to function. For example, patients can experience slow movement, memory impairment, confusion, heaviness, sleeplessness, restlessness, loss of focus, blurred vision and weight gain, among other effects. It is therefore critical that a psychiatrist listens to their patient's cry for help to determine how they can best help each other.

Even though I received my bipolar diagnosis in 1992, I only had my breakthrough in accepting my condition in March 2011. What made me come to grips with it was when Dr. Lacey was able to describe the things that I had gone through up to that moment. She did so without me sharing any of those details with her – she knew what was happening in my life during one of my episodes. I then realized that if this doctor knew what I was experiencing and could actually tell me, then indeed I did and do have bipolar. You see, not everyone can fully grasp or understand a condition unless they are personally experiencing it themselves, so it was eye-opening to have my doctor describe it in such detail.

In the past, there were times when I accepted the condition because the doctor said I had it, and then there were other times when I rejected my diagnosis because of who God said I am. I still believe in my own mental and physical strength, as ultimately God in His Word, 2 Timothy 1:7, says, "God did not give us a spirit of fear but of power, love and a sound mind." Because of that passage, I believe wholeheartedly in my ability to exercise soundness of mind, but I also believe my condition to be so. The key is that I do not surrender to it; otherwise, I would be stuck and unaccepting that God is in full control. Having said that, I also believe that if I was not spiritually connected, I could be worse. However, I acknowledge that it is only the grace of God that brings me through each time.

As I said before, I was always a natural leader, but because of my many bouts of illness and melancholy, I became a follower, as my inability to function crippled and suppressed my abilities. Nonetheless, I continued striving and thriving.

Questions:

1. What do you consider a mental illness?
2. Do you believe mental health patients should be handled by the police?
3. Do you think that family members should have their loved ones sanctioned?
4. What would you like to see happen if your family member had a mental health issue?
5. Do you believe that patients ought to be collected by nurses trained in mental health care instead of the police?
6. Do you think an institution is necessary for mental health patients?
7. Do you believe that the current facility in Cayman or in your hometown is sufficient?
8. Do you believe psychology, as opposed to psychiatry, should be the first priority for mental health patients?

CHAPTER 8

RELATIONSHIP, MARRIAGE AND FAMILY

I believe in pleasing and serving God. Although it can be difficult simply because we live in this world of sin, I thrive on learning how to submit to God first and foremost. I love being a nurturer, hospitable and a helpmate to my spouse. I enjoy attending church and a small group where I met a lovely group of ladies, who I call my "church sisters."

Some may think that being a housewife and mother is a lowly position. However, although men and women are created equal in God's sight, they nevertheless facilitate different roles. Each couple should prayerfully work out before the Lord how best they can complement and serve each other and their families. And as any single parent knows, one can often find themselves having to fulfil duties with which they dearly wish a partner was present and available to help. Each person should seek the wisdom, strength and help of the Lord, whether male or female, married or single.

I knew that I wanted a family, and that family life was very important to me, hence why I accepted a marriage proposal at the tender age of 26 years old. Although I wanted marriage, I was taken aback when it was proposed.

It was December 1990. I met Rob at a New Year's Eve party in Cayman! He and I dated for three months, and after that brief period, we were besotted. There and then we knew we wanted to be together forever.

I grew up financially secure, so I never had to worry about money, including at the time that Rob and I became friends. When Rob and I knew that we wanted to enter a long-term relationship, I invested

CI$10,000 into it, as Rob did not have much money. I recall our very first date – Rob paid for the first drink for us. When it was time for the second round, he looked at me and said, "Okay, now it is your turn."

Back then, ladies were used to men escorting them and paying for drinks and food too. I was flabbergasted when he proceeded to borrow CI$10 from me the very next day. "That was it," I said as I went back to the office and told my circle of friends. At work, my friends just loved getting reports and feedback about the weekend's happenings. They were happy to crowd my desk as I recalled events from my exciting days out of the office.

With an initial deposit of CI$10,000 – the investment I mentioned before – Rob and I were able to purchase a plot of land at Logwood Estates, which we later sold to make a profit of CI$30,000. Although we were from different backgrounds, races, cultures and religions, we knew that we wanted to give the relationship a good try, as we shared equal goals and values regarding marriage and starting a family. He was Catholic and I am Protestant. However, we thought that love conquered all.

I recall one of our dates on 14 February 1991. I was so excited, as it was Valentine's Day, and the dress I wore perfectly fit the red-and-white dress code for the occasion. I excitedly awaited Rob's arrival at my parents' house. The front door had a window through which one could peep outside. As I eagerly awaited his arrival, I peered through the window and was shocked to see Rob's appearance. He wore an undersized T-shirt with holes and white crushed jeans with frayed legs. I was not at all impressed. I quickly pulled Rob in and said, "I am sorry, but I cannot go with you dressed like that." He was equally surprised as I hurriedly looked for a red T-shirt that I asked him to wear instead. After all, I was all dressed and made up. The white jeep was also unimpressive, as it was dirty and filled with empty beer bottles and cans. Nevertheless, Rob and I had a great time at the party – another eventful and hilarious outing to report to my friends at the office on Monday.

As Rob and I continued dating, we became attached to one another, and he became my frequent companion to many parties and dinners. It was soon time for me to meet Rob's parents, as he had met mine and they immediately liked him, although my father had hang-ups because Rob was white. His mind reverted to the days of slavery, and he lamented how white people had treated black people. However, I did not let my father's feelings deter me from a relationship with Rob, and I decided to meet his parents as he wanted. He planned a trip to Connecticut, which would be my first visit there.

The flight took about four hours from Cayman to John F. Kennedy International Airport (JFK) in New York. There were direct flights to and from JFK. As soon as the plane landed, I became nervous knowing that Rob's parents awaited our arrival. When Rob spotted his parents, he pointed them out to me – and his mom's face dropped. His father was welcoming, but his mother was obviously disappointed. I knew immediately that it was not going to be a comfortable trip.

Fairfield, Connecticut, was about a two-hour drive from JFK. The conversation was very light as we all drove to Fairfield. I felt uneasy, but Rob's father, who was accommodating, made it quite comfortable, whilst his mom struggled to participate.

In Rob's parents' house, we were not allowed to co-habit. I was placed in a very nice and comfortable bedroom upstairs whilst Rob slept in the basement.

Rob had told me prior to meeting his parents that he could not let them know that we were an item. I asked why, but he was not forthcoming with the answer. I was rather uncomfortable and simply told Rob that I had to be myself, and I would normally and naturally ask his mother how she felt about our relationship. Still, I felt like I had to wear a disguise for the whole trip, so I took every opportunity I got to shop – it was the only thing that could take me away from my strange surroundings.

Back in Cayman, when my mother met Rob's parents, I experienced culture shock. Having met his American parents and being of Caymanian descent myself, the differences in religion, education and ethnicity were apparent and caused major issues. His mother's view was entirely different than ours, and I recall being dumbfounded and embarrassed when my mother was introduced to her. Even though his mother grew up on a farm and worked her way into a more affluent society, she appeared to have a supercilious nature. Nonetheless, out of love and respect for Rob, I stuck it out but found myself in a most comprising situation.

So, when Rob proposed marriage, I accepted. Rob and I got engaged in March 1991. He and I were to get married in September of that same year, but the wedding was put on hold when I suffered a nervous breakdown again and was hospitalized.

Dr. Fawn, who was from Jamaica and worked in Cayman in the 1990s, had formally labelled me as having bipolar affective disorder. Despite that, Rob and I had a very rich and beautiful courtship. He and I courted until June 1993, when we got married at St. Hugh's Catholic Church with family and friends in Miami, Florida.

It was a beautiful, sunny day as everyone prepared for the wedding. About 55 people had flown in from out of town, but the wedding party was quite small. There was one matron of honour, best man, flower girl and ring bearer. Catholic weddings were a new thing for me, mainly because we did not stand before the officiant – instead, we sat during the ceremony. The chapel was very small, quaint and lovely. Rob's uncle, Father Ray, was the officiant.

As I entered the church, the harpist played the song "Love in Any Language" as the guests stood up. Rob and I were both delighted to see each other! The ceremony lasted for only half an hour. After the service, the wedding party, together with family, left to take photographs in the garden of the main church. Reid McNeal, our photographer, was flown in from Cayman. He took beautiful photographs!

With the profit from the sale of the land we had previously purchased and a loan from one of Rob's former employers, Rob and I were able to purchase a family home on Selkirk Drive, Red Bay. With a gift from my father, we added a full-length porch to the rear of the house and a veranda to the front. Rob and I were happily settled in our new home, and we both had full-time jobs. What followed was a whirlwind: our daughter was born in 1994 and our son in 1996. I suffered postpartum depression with both children and was hospitalized. During that time, our children's caregiver, Carmen, and Rob looked after our daughter, Milena. That was a very busy and stressful year! However, I recovered and returned to work the following year. I had taken a year off to be a stay-at-home mom with each child and studied part-time at the International College of the Cayman Islands.

I had settled into family life, and everyone appeared happy, but my bouts of bipolar and frequent hospitalizations took me away from family. Because of the illness, seven years into the marriage, I wanted to leave, as I thought my absences were unfair to my husband and children. However, our neighbours came to our home to counsel us and asked me to stay in the marriage, as the children were little. Rob was not ready to let me go! Despite the ups and downs of my episodes, Rob and I enjoyed a very loving, fulfilling and happy marriage at first, for which we were envied by our friends. He and I shared and showed this love and affection openly, although I was still fighting with bipolar.

Marriage is a beautiful gift from God to embody the unity of His magnificent creation story, which begins in Genesis 1-3. It is symbolic of the communion between God the Father, the Son and the Holy Spirit, how they function and work as one. The unity between the three is never broken, and so it is with marriage. It is meant to be a lifelong union.

My consideration for marriage was based upon our commonalities and ideals: our belief in God, love, raising a family, school and finances. I committed to marriage in this relationship based on the unity between Rob's father and mother who, at the time, had been married for more than 30 years. The fact that Rob was a religious man was big for me; so was his stability in terms of responsibility, maturity and intent. However, this reasoning was not sufficient – later, I discovered that I had failed to consider many other facets, and the fact he went to church was not enough.

In my head, cultural differences were small compared to the love that Rob and I felt for each other. We knew we could overcome all obstacles! But what was a small thing for me became grandiose as we attempted to merge our families.

When a man and woman marry, although they are marrying each other, they are also marrying into extended families. Some people may disagree with this, but I have found it to be very true. On top of that, the mother-son bond is very important, and it can often be a determining factor in a split if his relationship causes a rift in the one with his mother. It is somewhat different for women because, although fathers get teary-eyed letting go of their daughters, eventually they hand them over and take a step back. It's not so easy with the mothers and sons, in my experience. Genesis 2:24 reminds us, "For this reason a man should leave his mother and be united to his wife and they shall become one flesh."

In the beginning, religion was no big deal because we both believed in God. Ha! Looking back, we were both ignorant in this area. Rob and I initially decided that we would get married in the Presbyterian church that I attended. However, we ended up marrying in a Catholic church. Once the children came along, all hell broke loose. The children were both baptized as Catholic and attended Catholic schools, and we all went to the Catholic church as a family. In the end, the schools were not necessarily a problem, but the choice of church was. Rob and I found ourselves in a tug-of-war.

Throughout the marriage, I had doubts about my belief in the Catholic church and could not convert. So, I danced between churches. Eventually, I ended up in a Baptist church. One of our disagreements was about splitting the children between the two religions. However, the best advice a pastor could have given me – which has stayed with me ever since – was, "Take the best of both." I went away feeling great about this. However, it did not go so well with Rob. It had to be Catholic all the way, as I uncovered later.

Some people ask, "What's love got to do with it?" Another popular cliché says, "Love is never having to say you are sorry." But I believe that love *is* about saying you are sorry every time you mess up. It is about staying the course when things do not go your way. It is about commitment – raising a family together and loving in tough times. It is about never giving up! Most importantly, love should be a reflection of God. It meant all or nothing to me. It was to be my lifelong commitment to God, my family and myself.

I always believed in fairy tales. Some may call this hopeless, but I saw it as seeking something never-ending. I truly meant it when I said, "Until death do we part." It will not always be pretty, but the outcome, in the end, is a satisfying and rewarding journey of an interwoven life well spent together. Although I did want to walk away once, staying the course was of paramount importance – I never believed in divorce and still do not. Leaving a marriage would not be an easy task, except in the case of infidelity and/or adultery. Whether I was poor or rich would not be a deterrent for a marriage. It is nice to have money, but money should not rule over a relationship or be a determining factor for it to continue or end. When the going gets tough and money is short, relationships not based on Godly leadership will often fail.

Rob and I both had strong beliefs about family. Leaving my family behind would have been one of the hardest things for me to do, especially leaving my children. I did not believe I would have had the gall to leave, even if things were desperately bad. My strong beliefs about family would have overridden any desire to leave.

It is often said that marriage is a two-way street. I believe that a stronger metaphor for marriage is that it takes two to tango. Marriage is a lifelong commitment to a partner. It is not a conditional union, but rather an unconditional one instituted by God. It is not something to take lightly, and there are many factors that should be considered before a marriage takes place. For example, do you both have a relationship with Christ? If so, are you on the same page? Do you want children? Are you ready for a lifelong commitment? There are so many other intricate questions and answers pertaining to marriage that can and should be taken into consideration – even race, religion and cultural relationships on which people often do not see eye to eye. I came to realize these truths later in my first marriage.

My first mistake was to make a commitment to marriage based on someone else's relationship – Rob's mother's and father's. This, you will discover, was not enough for us to stay married. On top of that, I learned that one ought to make a commitment not solely based on love and comfort, but one with God being central in the decision-making process. If He is not, this is a mistake that can easily lead to divorce. Although Christian marriages fail sometimes, I do not believe that God was central in my marriage, either. God's love is unconditional, so I believe that counsel ought to come from God, rather than relying on ourselves for advice. As noted in Galatians 5:16, when we gratify the desires of the flesh, we are prone to blatant sin. When we please the spiritual nature, we are seeking things of the Spirit. Marriage should be based upon the relationship with God first and foremost, and then the relationship between the couple, just as God intended.

Your background is a significant part of being in a committed relationship, as it is very much a part of who you are as a person. This should not be ignored, as you will draw on your own experiences and beliefs when financial troubles, mental health issues and other problems creep up.

In my view, religion does play a great role. Imagine a marriage that merges two different religions, and yet both people continue to act independently. Each wants to put forward their beliefs as well as their customs. This is a battleground for disagreements and major arguments. So it says in the Bible, "Do not be unequally yoked." This means that a believer shouldn't be married to a non-believer, as the two do not have anything in common: one is for God and the other acts contrary to the laws of God. I believe this is true, especially in my experience. It's extremely hard when one person believes something totally different from their spouse.

I often tell myself and believe that love is all or nothing! You cannot have one foot in the door and the other out. Love is an action and decision that is as all-inclusive and unconditional as God is. Love is infinite, and so is the Church and God. He is love, and that's why unions based on God's love succeed.

A man committed to God first and to you second would definitely cling to you and stay in a marriage. If that man is truly dedicated to Christ, then He will be faithful and loving to his wife. He will cherish her and honor her as he does the Lord. Whatever is true, noble, right, pure and praiseworthy, the union will thrive on these virtues, as expressed in Philippians 4:8.

I believe that although money is necessary for basic needs, it is not a means to an end. Loving in tough times as well as good times is the key, with the couple focusing on God, who ultimately provides. Two are better than one, in terms of companionship. If you have love and no money, love will keep you warm, but money comes and goes. Money is not bad. It is the love of it that is the root of all evil, according to 1 Timothy 6:10. So, having money cannot buy you love. With God central in your house, love conquers all.

Seeking Godly counsel before the going gets tough and adhering to Godly principles is key to a successful marriage. Although I tried leaving, I would not have abandoned my home, my marriage or my children, as I believed in marriage. In good or bad situations, with Christ, all things are possible, including overcoming marriage difficulties. Abandoning marriage is basically leaving behind and giving up on those you love and to whom you were committed. I believed that I could not give up on my family, particularly my children.

Reconciliation is great, but it is a very difficult thing to do. There are trust issues and a lack of transparency, as well as one constantly having to look over their shoulder, waiting for their partner's wrong moves. I would only consider reconciliation in certain instances; namely, if both parties agreed to put God central in their union. Marriages based on biblical truths and actions often last for a very long time – until death do the couple part.

I would encourage anyone wishing to be married to seek God's guidance first: pray and put Him above every decision in your life. Whether it is relationship, finances, differences, beliefs, anything – take it to God.

"Therefore I tell you, do not worry about your life, what you will eat or drink; or about your body, what you will wear. Is not life more than food..."
– Matthew 6:25-33

Questions:

1. How would you define marriage?
2. On what grounds would you make a commitment?
3. Do you believe background is an important factor?
4. Do you believe religion would make a difference in marriage?
5. What does love mean to you?
6. What do you believe would make you stay the course? What would make you leave a marriage?
7. Do you believe financial matters play a big role in a marriage?
8. Would abandoning your home be a solution to marital problems?
9. Do you believe in divorce? If so, on what grounds?
10. Do you believe in reconciliation? If so, on what grounds?
11. Do you believe that God should be central in marriage?

CHAPTER 9

BROKENNESS

SEPARATION

The day Rob abandoned the family home – and took our children with him – was the greatest grief for me. I bawled like a baby. He hit me where it hurt most by taking my children away from me.

My children were nine and seven at the time; it was just when my daughter was about to experience puberty. Without a doubt, it must have been an incredibly hard and lonely period for her, a time when she would really need her mother's guidance. I mourned the loss not only of my children, but of Rob and the family unit that we had so valiantly built. Our love for each other was displayed publicly. Even with the trials we faced, I assumed that this love would conquer all. Unfortunately, it did not. That is why God's love should be central in any relationship.

DIVORCE

Divorce separates lives and hurts the couple who's splitting, as well as others in their lives. I do not believe in divorce, as it is not God's design. When children are involved, it is even worse – it is psychologically damaging and painful. Not only are you splitting up with your family, but you are also breaking sacred vows. A marriage is a partnership and binding union, which is not to be taken lightly. Some people get married for the wrong reasons. You should not base love and marriage solely on principles. It takes more than that to sustain a marriage. And, again, divorce creates all kinds of hardships; however, I would leave a marriage if there were extramarital affairs.

I became ill again in April 2003 and was hospitalized but released early. Rob began to act very strangely toward me. Events happened so fast! However, our anniversary was around the corner. Rob and I celebrated 10 years of marriage with a beautiful weekend getaway to Cayman Brac. Two months after that, I was served papers for a divorce. I was shocked – this was totally unexpected! So were a handful of friends once they learned of us getting a divorce. You see, Rob was divorcing me based on irreconcilable differences, stemming from the fact that he believed I was ill and could not manage my illness. However, sickness is not something one can control – it's a part of life. No one intentionally becomes ill. It may take time, but it's better to be patient than exacerbate someone's stress.

The divorce proceedings became very difficult, bitter and unpleasant. By this time, Rob had taken the children, abandoned the family home and denied me access to my son and daughter through the courts. This was really tearing me apart, as I loved being a mother more than anything. Rob – on behalf of himself and my kids – put a restraining order against me, and that came as a massive insult. There was certainly no basis for it. He wanted me ousted from the home that we had shared for more than ten years.

My daughter and son were raised by both parents to ages nine and seven, respectively. Going from normal parenting to supervised time with them was awful! It was obvious that my ex-husband was manipulating the children and ostracizing me from them. When my daughter had to be left with me, she would cry for no apparent reason. I had to get a friend to come over to console her.

Financially, Rob left me bankrupt. During the marriage, we had decided that he would pay the bills and I would save my salary for the marriage. I gave him my pay check every month, except when I purchased both family vehicles. Rob and I invested in stocks, totalling up to CI$52,000. He sold them just prior to filing for divorce. This was discovered after the fact, so I received nothing from the proceeds! He and I were jointly on the mortgage account. Rob told me that he needed to take me off for tax purposes, but that he would continue to pay the mortgage. I did not agree! Little did I know, he was planning to take the house for himself. However, the judge did not believe that he should receive the house in a split of our assets. He and I had also purchased a piece of land in East End, on which we had owed the bank some CI$40,000. I did not receive the house free and clear, but acquired quite a liability – some CI$160,000. Meanwhile, Rob received the land by the end of the proceedings.

During one of my hospitalizations, Rob shut down all our bank accounts and opened new accounts in his name (and one in his and his mother's names), cutting me off from our finances. One of the documents served to me with the divorce papers was an affidavit, and I found its contents baffling, hurtful and not at all in line with the love I thought we had for one another, especially because it appeared to be a well-planned document. Rob's family stopped communicating with me just prior to the divorce, and this continued during and after the proceedings. Apparently, they knew of his intentions! Rob had others believing that I was "crazy" and needed to be hospitalized at a time when I did not need to be and was declared fit by my then-psychiatrist.

Days before separation, Rob and I had a minor disagreement about who would take the children to church: him or me. This ended with a verbal battle. He then called the cops and tried to have me put in the hospital. Rob did not have his way that time and he was furious!

I was simply fed up, as this was going to be a long and embarrassing process. I would have preferred a settlement out of court. However, I was being treated unfairly not only by Rob, but by the system too. Although the Department of Children and Family Services was briefly involved, I knew the system did not handle matters properly, nor did they conduct any real or thorough investigation into the family's background during the divorce. Therefore, there were all kinds of loopholes that I did not understand, as Rob would not talk to me at all, before or during the whole process. I was exhausted and spent – getting a divorce alone was a surprise!

In 2004, when the divorce was finalized, Rob tried boldly and arrogantly speaking to me. I was livid. How dare he? This time, I lost it, as I could not figure out what would happen with my access to my children, nor could I fathom why this man was getting away with so much.

As reiterated, I do not believe in divorce, nor had I considered it. I thought that marrying Rob would be enough for me and that it would be a forever thing. I always assumed that we were on the same page and knew where matters of the heart stood. Divorce breaks relationships and builds walls that shouldn't be torn down, let alone exposed to the world.

Questions:

1. Have you ever considered divorce?
2. Do you think that divorce is harmful?
3. On what grounds would you separate or divorce?
4. Do you believe that when you divorce, you are divorcing your children as well as your spouse?
5. Is divorce harmful to children?
6. Do you believe divorce separates friends on both sides?
7. Are there any nice divorces?
8. Does God like divorce?
9. Is divorce healthy?
10. How would you split your assets if you were divorcing your spouse?

CHAPTER 10

WOUNDED AND IN JAIL

I believe that some cops in Cayman during those times, and even still today, are a mess and a disgrace to the Royal Cayman Islands Police Service, as they manhandle innocent mental health patients. They are barbaric and crude, preying on people who are often already ill-treated. Cayman's mental health system, as it is today, dispatches cops to handle mental health patients. At the same time, the cops improperly treat innocent people who need care. The government of the day is aware of this but blatantly ignores it. I recall that, because of this unfair treatment, a Caymanian gentleman went after one of his psychiatrists with a gun, and he left the Islands shortly afterwards.

In February 2004, an uncharacteristic incident took place in my life, too. I was so angry that I gave way to the devil! He took complete control, even after I had reconciled my relationship with God in January 2004. That was one month before the incident, the one in which I decided to take matters into my own hands by attempting to kill Rob, after which I planned to end my own life. However, this was not God's plan, as he interceded. I stabbed Rob once, but I knew that I could not go through with the rest – God stopped me short. I heard a small voice say, "Don't do it." Rob and I then had a struggle, and we both agreed to ease up and drop the weapon. I questioned Rob, wondering, "Why did you act so?" All he said was that he was sorry.

I then drove him to the hospital. There and then, I was asked, "What happened?" I immediately confessed that I had stabbed him. I was instantly arrested and jailed for eight days without bail.

I found myself incarcerated on 8 February 2004, at the George Town Police Station, just four days after my messy divorce had been completed.

In jail, I was placed in a cold, damp cell with only a slab of cement for a bed. I wept and mourned for the loss of my children and asked God to take away that worry. The cell reeked of urine and faeces. There was neither bedding nor pillows to make it more comfortable. I curled up in a foetal position, which kept me warm. The cells were situated far from the main entrance, so no one could hear me from my cell – that is, unless I hollered for help. Even then, I had to wait until the officer was good and ready to come to my aid.

I had never envisioned going to prison prior, during or even after committing the crime. Prison is something most people don't think about unless they know someone in the prison system, whether they are incarcerated within it or employed by it.

Many times, I had to urinate or defecate right where I was for lack of help to get to the facilities. Sometimes, there was no toilet paper. When I was allowed to go, I would hear the officer coming down the corridor with keys jingling, ready to let me out, but I usually didn't even need to go. I would often give in to the urge long before an officer would respond to me.

I dreaded shower time because the water was so cold. There was no hot water. After shower time, I would prepare myself to curl back up on the slab of cement. Most days and nights, I did not sleep. I started singing Christian songs that would comfort me.

I was in jail until 13 February 2004, before my transfer to HMP Fairbanks Prison, which housed female prisoners. By that time, Rob had gotten full custody, care and control of the children.

PRISON

On that day, two officers – a male and female – came to receive me. It was a rule that if there was a female prisoner, you had to have a female officer as an escort. I was handcuffed and taken out of the police car. I was relieved to see sunlight, as it had been dreary in the jail.

It was a sad and lovely day! It was sad because I was going to real prison, and I had heard dreadful stories about female prisoners. Lovely, because it was a beautiful day, the weather was fair, and I was finally getting to see real sunlight! The drive between jail and prison took about five minutes.

Upon arrival, I was handed over to a fierce-looking Haitian female officer. There was not even a smile or any greeting. As I proceeded up the walkway, I looked over my shoulder in time to see the police vehicle driving off. With that, the prison would become my home for quite a while. To start, I would be on remand for four months before the trial was to begin. I faced one charge of attempted murder, and I was sentenced to 12 years' imprisonment. I later appealed, and my sentence was reduced to 8 years, of which I spent 32 months in prison.

Once inside on my first day, I was greeted by two officers: Beaver, a tall, elegantly dressed officer; and Daisy, who was shorter with bowlegs. I was relieved to see Daisy, who was a cousin of my mother's and a second mother to me. Nevertheless, she had a duty to fulfil, and she could not show any partiality to me.

During my time at the jail, I had collected some personal items from my extended family. However, they were confiscated and taken away in a large garbage bag. I was then ushered in to remove my clothes. Then, I was given a green prison uniform. I was a prisoner!

I was escorted to the southeast side of the prison, where I was placed in maximum security. On my walk there, I went through the main area where the dining and TV room were located – and other female prisoners looked on.

In maximum security, there were three cells. There were two other inmates, so it was full. Every morning, the officers woke us up to take showers. The shower stalls were situated north of the cell; it was public for all the female prisoners. I was so relieved when I'd get the one shower with hot water. There were about four shower stalls.

My first day in maximum security was scary and miserable. All I wanted to do was sleep. I curled up on the thin metal bed and mattress and clung to my Bible. I was simply tired and needed much rest. At the time, I was not medicated, so I was happy to be able to function and retain passages from the Bible that would help me pass the day.

I looked up toward the ceiling and thought about the days ahead. Everything up to that point in my life had happened so fast! The changes had caught up with me. All I could think of was being knocked out. I felt that everything I was experiencing was not actually happening to me.

I had arrived at the prison in the afternoon. I had missed lunch and was the only prisoner in maximum security at that time. I was so tired that I did not hear when the officer came to bring supper. I was not even hungry! I was restless, as sleep did not come easily.

In the entire prison, there were about 24 female inmates. The inside of the prison was shaped like a rectangle with an inner square of chicken wire fence, which created a space called the day room, where you'd find a single TV. Outside of the wired fence, we had space to walk around the entire rectangle. The dorms lined its perimeter. There were four dorms in total, simply referred to as dorm 1, 2, 3 and 4. Juvenile prisoners would generally be housed in dorm 4.

The classroom/library was situated at the southern end of the prison. On the north end, you'd find the entrance, waiting area and staff office. Then, there was the kitchen, which sat across from the storeroom and lead officer's office.

The prison looked like an old run-down house, complete with a scanty garden. A tall fence with coiled barbed wire at the top surrounded the rear yard. In my earlier days, I had tried escaping by climbing the fence, but Officer Daisy rescued me.

Before my downfall, I had never, ever thought of prison. But two weeks before I ended up behind bars, I had carelessly said to my father, "He [Rob] better mind if I go to prison for him." Little did I know that this statement would cause so much pain and regret. This was when I really discovered that "life and death is in the power of the tongue," as stated in Proverbs 18:21. I did not for a second consider or think that I would have committed a crime after saying something like that. I had never even thought of breaking the law! So, there was no reaction to the thought of prison until I actually got there. That moment still did not sink in until days later – I was in shock.

After I drove Rob to the hospital, I confessed the crime I committed, so I did not have to acknowledge this further to anyone. Sometime after I was transferred to the female prison, I received a visit from a so-called close friend, who bluntly told me that I had committed a crime in cold blood. I just looked and stared, as I felt so flabbergasted. One just does not commit a crime for no reason – there is always a root cause. I quickly realized that I was no killer or dreadful slayer, just someone whose emotions became overwhelming in the heat of the moment.

VISITATION

My sister Claire and her friend Katie visited me faithfully each week. I looked forward to seeing them every time, as these visits brought me such a sense of relief.

I did not realize the finality of what had occurred and where I would end up – as I said, I was in shock. Prison is a place where not only your rights are taken away, but your dignity as well. You are told exactly what to do and where, when and how. Decisions are not made by you, but for you. I believe that recidivism is so high because many prisoners become co-dependent in prison. Depending on the length of their sentences, some people leave prison with an inability to cope on their own anymore.

Prison life is rigid, and it is supposed to be structured. However, in Cayman, every officer abides by their own rules, so it isn't as regimented as in other places. They simply do not follow protocol. Consistency appeared to be routine in terms of daily activities; for example, wake-up and shower times. Finding routine in any other activities was like pulling teeth. They never served lunch on time. Classes were always being postponed. The officers conducted random searches when they had suspicions. They ignored our requests for medical help more often than not. However, once the officers did get around to taking me to the hospital, I was shackled and handcuffed. Those times were difficult and embarrassing.

CHAPTER 11

PROTECTION FOR MY CHILDREN

Before going to prison, while dealing with the divorce, the only thing I could think of was protecting my children. I could not be certain that they would have been cared for by Rob because of what had transpired and the rapid decline of my family.

It was about 4am. The children and I were in our beds. I was restless, preoccupied with all that was happening in the divorce proceedings. I could only focus on that and making a way out; I felt I was being trapped. I got up and took a pen and pad to the bathroom. I wrote about four or five pages, making provisions for my children in the form of a suicide letter. I was told after the later proceedings for attempted murder that this was why I had received such a lengthy sentence – because of intent. Sometime later, I tried to drift off to sleep but I could not. However, I had a few books by my bedside, one of which was a book by T.D. Jakes, *Woman Thou Art Loosed*. I thought I would find comfort in reading this book, which I did. But my mind still would revert to the difficulties ahead. "What am I to do?" I asked myself.

As dawn came, I threw together Rob's belongings. I telephoned him, asking him to pick them up. The thoughts just kept playing over and over in my mind: how he had gotten away with so much, how embarrassed and ashamed I was. I thought we could have settled out of court, but no – he wanted to see me destroyed. His behaviour when he arrived to gather his things was my last straw. He came in arrogantly and wanted to have a conversation with me. I thought, "How dare you!" This was the same man who would not even acknowledge me during the whole ordeal. If I went to the left, he would go to the right. In the end, he treated me like trash! The court did not see this, nor would they have taken it into consideration; the treatment, the brokenness, the mental abuse and the frustrations of dealing with a family that had it all together, save for my bouts of bipolar disorder.

When I told the judge in court that there was absolutely no correlation between my bipolar disorder and the crime I committed, the judge was astonished and thought I should not have said that. However, this could not be further from the truth. I simply just lost it!

I recall when it was all finished, the reaction was no reaction at all. I was just numb. I could not feel anything. Even when I first appeared in court, I was numb.

Having been through this ordeal and committing a crime, I would say to anyone, first and foremost, seek God and sincere Godly people. When you are going through difficulties, your so-called friends are the first to go, and extended family can be so caught up in their own lives that it is difficult to become involved or empathize with somebody else's problems and pain. When you feel trapped and have nowhere to turn, no one can pull you through but God.

Friends come and friends go. Those genuine friends who know you best are the ones you should really pursue. On the other hand, it really hurts to be treated callously by someone who has been beside you most of your life, but who sees you commit a crime and describes it as "done in cold blood." If a friend says something so hurtful and untrue, keep in mind that they probably did not know you at all.

Being a strong woman, believing in God and accepting His forgiveness means all is not lost. When situations and people seem grim, God never leaves you or forsakes you.

Going to prison was a life-altering experience. I am not proud of going to prison, but I am happy that the grace of God kept me from despair.

Questions:

1. Have you ever envisioned going to prison? What do you think your reaction would be?
2. Have you ever thought of committing a crime?
3. What would you say to family or friends afterwards?
4. How would you respond to a close friend who judged you after you committed a crime?
5. If you were in prison, would you consider all to be lost?
6. What would you say to your children or spouse, if anything?
7. How would you speak to the person you hurt?
8. Would you continue a relationship with your children during your time in prison?
9. Do you believe that children should visit you in prison if you are incarcerated?

CHAPTER 12

COUNSEL

I had retained an attorney. His name was Mr. Toby. Toby was a short, no-nonsense kind of a man who did not have any background in criminal law, as his area of practice was commercial litigation and insolvency. I had chosen Toby because I had worked with him for eight years at a law firm. Toby thought he could handle the case and brought on board his colleague, Mr. Nicky.

I had my first questioning by Nicky in the jail. He sought approval for representation on my behalf. I vaguely remember what was said, but I did know he was working with Toby that day.

The detailed questioning took quite some time, as I had to give my witness statement. The session took place in a private room upstairs in the police building. I was further questioned by a police officer, Mr. Jones, and a female officer. He had a series of questions that I answered whilst the lady officer looked on. I told them exactly what had occurred leading up to the incident. As I spoke, I sobbed like a baby. The whole ordeal was heart-wrenching, particularly once I was arrested. I was stripped down in front of other officers, and photos were taken of me naked. I was so ashamed.

COUNSELLOR

Opportunity is something to be grasped. For example, when someone is trying to help you out of a messy situation, take hold of it, for you will reap the benefits – benefits that do not come easily. So often we miss good opportunities because we believe that we are self-sufficient. However, God did not place us in this world to be self-sufficient – he wants us to be totally dependent upon him. We live in a world where everything is "me"-focused, which is not how it's supposed to be. We are called to put God and others first.

Freedom is having peace that passes all understanding, as documented in Philippians 4:7. God promises us that if we are obedient to him, we shall experience this peace. By His grace, we can have peace. I believe and have witnessed that it is possible to experience God's peace in all circumstances, even when you are deep down in the valley.

There are people who come into your life on a professional basis who you wish had not even dared to do so. However, there are those who, from the very beginning, make you feel that they genuinely wish to help. I met Mike Chester, a former counsellor at the Cayman Islands Counselling Centre, in 2005 at HMP Fairbanks, the women's prison where I was incarcerated. I had seen him at the hospital on the mental health inpatient unit as a nurse. I didn't know Mr Chester then – and I didn't see him on the unit for very long – but I later found out that he had gotten a transfer to the counselling centre.

In his role as counsellor, Mr. Chester had to visit both prisons in Cayman. Every Tuesday, he would show himself at the prison. He told me why he was there, and thus began our counsellor-counselee relationship. I very much enjoyed our meetings, as this was a time for someone to really listen to me. The sessions started with the basics: my background, the incident with Rob, mental health, family and prison life.

Mr. Chester was a very keen listener. He would recap everything from the previous week, as most counsellors should, although some have a hard time keeping track and don't have much to say in response. Chester and I had a good working relationship. I looked forward to Tuesdays, as I would get to share my thoughts and alleviate the tension and stress of the week.

This relationship continued even after I got out of prison. Mr. Chester faithfully counselled me on a weekly basis. I was so grateful to have met him, as he genuinely cared for his clients.

CHAPTER 13

CRIME

Having been on both sides – working in a law firm and then becoming part of the criminal system – I found myself eagerly wanting to help prisoners, my community and the government. I realized that what I had to contribute was critical and relevant to lessen and even prevent crime in Caymanian society.

Before being in the criminal system, I had a reputable character, one that was admired and praised by my peers, family and the community at large. I had overcome many challenges in my life, faced setbacks and made mistakes. However, it did not change who I was and what I believed to be good and true about myself and, very importantly, the things God affirmed about me. Today, I am still that person – confident, poised and determined, someone who has overcome struggles, resentment, rejection, labels and difficulties presented by my circumstances. In my mind, I never saw these problems as a deterrent to living a good life, but rather as an opportunity to improve on the person I was, and reclaim the positive view and good character that others and I knew that I possessed. I do not see myself as a dangerous woman, as some may think. Rather, I see myself as a loving wife, mother and friend who has had a complex life, stemming from inner struggles as well as external forces.

Something is drastically wrong in our society. Crime happens everywhere, although in some places it is more prevalent than in others. However, for the sake of my story, I want to focus on crime in Cayman.

Crime is elemental. It takes root. Therefore, it must start from somewhere, from some problem. In my opinion and in my own experience, the judicial system, the government and the community need to get to the root of the problem. This can aptly be done with the proper punishment and treatment of those who have committed crimes. Too much time and energy are spent on "more" punishment without us genuinely uncovering the root cause of crime – and figuring out how to remedy it.

For example, let's say you know of a person who has lived a crime-free life and suddenly something wrong happens in that person's life, which causes them to go to prison. Or perhaps there's someone who lives in a bad neighbourhood surrounded by crime. Or maybe a person is simply caught up in a bad situation, one in which that person ends up in prison. These scenarios do not mean that these people are criminals and will continue to live in that state. But society will view each of those people as "bad", "dangerous", a "prisoner" etc., without considering their character before the misfortune.

I have been on both sides of the fence. I know that on the "good" side, hearing the word "prison" or "prisoner" was a very negative thing because, like you, I assumed everyone who went to prison was simply a bad person. However, once I found myself on the "bad" side, I realized that good people make mistakes, and not everyone who goes to prison is necessarily "bad" or "criminal". I am not proud that I have been to prison, and I take full responsibility for my actions. I believe in justice and punishment, and I also believe that there is a better way to reduce crime and diminish the rate of recidivism.

In Cayman, the population is very small. As such, there is a comparatively small body of representatives and police on the Islands who know the locals and their backgrounds – criminals or prisoners included. Should wrongdoers be punished? Yes! But essentially, I think we need to start getting to the root of the problem, work with each individual to restore them back to the position they were in before the crime happened. There is often unfair treatment on these Islands, wherein criminals and prisoners are befriended by some high-society folks. This should not be the case, but unfortunately, many recidivists fall prey to this kind of incontestable situation, one that can even be ignored by some judges.

Another issue is how we treat someone who has been released from prison. Do not compound the problem by labelling, denying privileges or rejecting that person from society, particularly when they have positively restored their life. When someone serves their time, isn't that enough? Society shouldn't continue the punishment – leave judgment to the Lord.

Here is a thought: I likened this crime situation to that of a mother scolding her child for "bad" behaviour. In good, ethical homes, once the child's punishment is over, the mother reminds the child of the wrong done, corrects the child's behaviour, and affirms and assures the child of her love for them. She doesn't continue to tell the child they are "bad" over and over, as this will indeed justify future negative actions. In other words, with negative reinforcement, the child will do it again.

On the other hand, the child that is corrected and affirmed after punishment will be in a better position and is unlikely to repeat their actions. In the grand scheme of things, recidivism operates in the same fashion: you will have repeat offenders if they are not exposed to good values and principles, as well as opportunities to improve. That's why continuing to treat released prisoners as criminals is counter-productive and will likely exacerbate crime in the community.

THE SOLUTION

I want to see crime cease, but let's face it, crime will never be completely erased from any society. However, it can be significantly reduced and become less burdensome and costly. To prevent crime as much as possible, we need to support each other. A role model can get to know a would-be criminal or former prisoner and set an example for what their life could be. Any one of us could become that role model. I suggest you get to know the positives in the other person's life, encourage them, be involved and help set the course for their life after prison so that they don't stay down. Always remember not to judge prisoners. You don't know that person's story; you don't know why that person was so driven. And you should give them the space and opportunity to change.

PAROLE

I was blessed to be assigned to Mrs. Riley, who is a probation officer at the Probation and Aftercare Unit. Mrs. Riley is a quiet but assured young woman who is very caring and thorough; I instantly took a liking to her.

Because of my experiences in prison – feeling as though I was being attacked and torn down at every turn – I thought that I would not be given parole. However, God did not give up on me. He saw fit that it was time for me to leave prison, as He had finished His work in that phase of my life. I was anxious to leave, as I had grown tired of being locked away and feeling unable to move forward with my plans for a better life.

Therefore, in August 2006, I wrote the following letter to the parole board seeking release after two days of learning the parole procedures and release:

Dear Parole Panel,

As I reflect over the past two days, I wonder: What is parole? Who is eligible? And what does it mean to me? I find myself eagerly anticipating a chance to re-enter society.

Am I really ready?

What prison has meant for me over the past 32 months may be something entirely different from the few recidivists' experiences I have seen during this period.

Being on the other side of the fence, hearing the word "prison" was a very negative thing; I assumed that those who went to prison were simply "bad" people. However, being on this side of the fence, I've realized that bad things happen to good people, and not everyone who goes to prison is necessarily bad.

I am not proud that I am in prison. I take full responsibility for my actions, and I believe that I have paid the consequences. I am extremely sorry for the hurt caused to family, friends and society at large.

However, as I have been a part of the problem, I would like an opportunity to be part of the solution. I hope to align myself with members of the Probation and Aftercare Unit, fellow former inmates and young people in order to reduce crime and the rate of recidivism that is so prevalent, particularly amongst those young people.

Should I be granted parole, I promise to meet the requirements and recommendations set out by the board and return to being a productive member of society in order to alleviate the burden placed on our judicial system.

Questions for Released Prisoners and Parolees:

1. While you were in prison, did you make any constructive plans for life after your release? What were they?
2. If you were to end up back in prison, what policies or systems would you like to see implemented that were not there before?
3. Would you like to see changes in your life, or are you happy with the way you are living now?
4. What advice would you give to a young prisoner?
5. Would you like to be a part of the solution to your problems?
6. Do you see your life as problematic?
7. How would you like to bring about change?

BUILDING MORE PRISONS

On release, there was an article in the local newspaper that I read with much interest. It announced the building of a bigger prison, and it also made the argument that we needed a juvenile detention facility.

Firstly, I believe that Cayman does not need a bigger prison, nor does it need a juvenile detention facility to house more would-be criminals. Secondly, the fact that the government was looking into spending millions of dollars on such a project would be futile and counterproductive. Thirdly, the proposed facilities came to be based on speculation that crime would continue to be a huge factor in our society in the coming years, so it was better to be prepared. And lastly, the article contained no concrete solution or focus on reducing crime and the rate of recidivism so that we wouldn't need such additions to our prison system.

Society needs a correctional facility, but we also need to focus and enhance the existing halfway house by improving its standards. Prison is not a solution – it is only confinement from society. Our youths need help in a progressive way, not punishment that pushes them into a regressive state.

The fact that building new, larger prisons would be futile and counterproductive is backed by the saying, "If you build it, more will come." Take, for example, the fact that back in the 80s or early 90s, Cayman had very few security guards. Entering the new millennium, Cayman had a great influx of security guards. Only then did it seem there was a boost in criminality – robberies, thefts, burglaries and violence – compared to previous years.

Criminals are already being punished, so why focus on housing more of them? Cayman needs constructive ways of improving their lives and deterring would-be criminals.

Society needs to give hope and encouragement that there is a better way of life. Some of these so-called criminals are not given a chance because of the label they receive after prison.

Criminal justice systems need to get to the root of the problem because far too much emphasis is placed on the *actus reus*, i.e. what has gotten the person in trouble. Many such acts could have been prevented if we had punishment to deter criminals in place.

As there is class stratification (poor, middle and upper classes) in any society, you will always have people grappling for improvement and trying to push others out of the way to achieve their means, although there are some who are content in their status.

Having said that, firstly, I believe that the government in most jurisdictions – particularly in mine – has caused the influx of crime. When you look back some 35 or 40 years, crime was not a big issue here. Yes, we have a different Cayman today! However, if you look at the amount of control that our government has given to foreign leaderships in disciplining our young people, there is no wonder why we have a huge crime problem.

Firstly, for example, Caymanians are used to disciplining their children in a more structured way than some foreign nationals, particularly those from outside of the Caribbean region. They tend to be more lenient with doling out punishment to their children. I believe that is why you have a huge crime issue in some American and European countries and other larger nations.

Secondly, you might find that this discipline is misplaced. It is not at all parallel, nor is it stringent enough for children. People who repeatedly commit crimes start from a very young age. Children thrive on good, genuine discipline, so receiving weak or wavering punishments won't help them grow.

Furthermore, the government contributes largely to these crimes in some instances, and our judicial system is a player in this, too. Lastly, there are always two sides to a story – and, at times, there are more than two sides. There are serious reasons why these crimes are being committed, much to the detriment of some innocent persons. But desperation can cause crime, too.

Questions:
1. What would you consider a crime?
2. Do you believe that crime is a major issue in our society?
3. How would you handle crime?
4. Do you think crime should be punishable after a certain age?
5. Does crime affect everyone?

CHAPTER 14

CRIMINOLOGY

I think about the way in which crime is defined and categorized in jurisdictions the world over. Not everyone who commits a crime is a criminal. "Criminal," as it stands today, should be categorized and construed differently. For example, theft, dishonesty, money laundering and embezzlement constitute criminal activity.

But there are also times when the criminal justice system is discriminatory, prejudicial and anachronistic in nature. I stress again that not everyone who goes to jail or prison is necessarily a criminal.

I further declare that judicial systems the world over need to focus on key areas that need revamping and prioritize what is necessary for good governance and progress. The term "criminal" needs to be re-examined, as not every prisoner is a criminal, and there are many forms of differentiation of wrongdoing under the term.

Whilst in prison, I became instrumental in many areas, and I used the time to better myself, too. I served as a librarian, acquired a business management diploma, oversaw the facility's hurricane preparedness kits and kept fit by doing daily physical activities. To prepare myself to re-enter society, I wrote business plans. For example, I outlined an idea to create a halfway house, property maintenance business and guest house. On that note, I also utilized my time well by focusing and working on what I wanted to achieve.

This plan did work for me in my own home. While in prison, I also knew I wanted to work for a property maintenance and renovations company. I accomplished my goals and much more, as I immediately received a job after my release, which allowed me to open the guest house later. God has certainly been gracious and good to me. In turn, I have also helped a few teenagers as well as women in difficult circumstances, as there were quite a few recidivists, and I wanted to help prevent that. I read many books as well as the Bible on a daily basis.

Given the opportunity, I would put a Bible in each person's hands to help them the way it helped me. I believe that prisons in Cayman need to be more regimented in terms of preparing prisoners to lead productive lives upon release, as rehabilitative orders are insufficient and unreliable. In my view, the best way to do this is to pair prisoners with role models; it should be like holding their hands to guide them to successful rehabilitation. Too many times, upon release, they are left to the same company as before – or they are alone.

Anyone would love to see positive changes in their life, particularly if their lifestyle goes against what society considers decent. While in prison, I knew right away that I needed to do something to stay sane, be productive and prepare myself to re-enter society. I was not going to stay down; instead, I would reclaim who I knew myself to be as intended by God, and I was going to be successful in every area of my life.

I now see the benefits of living and leading a positive, fulfilling, productive life. Negativity will keep anyone in a rut. Who wants to live life in the doldrums? Not me!

My advice to prisoners would be to make the best of your circumstances. Although your freedom is taken away, you can have freedom in Christ. Make use of your time – do not waste it! You will never have that time back again. Prisoners have a lot of time on their hands to be the best of themselves and prove to society that they can make a difference. They can change and lead productive lives. First and foremost, I would encourage prisoners to read the book of life, the Bible, so that they know who they are, whose they are, and to put God in all things. This is the key to successful living!

As I wrote to the parole board, I wanted to be given an opportunity to be part of the solution and not continue being part of the problem. I knew before my incarceration that I was a good person who had just re-committed my life to Christ. However, if you take your eyes off Him and fix them on your circumstances, you will be heading for trouble, and that is exactly what happened to me. I would say to anyone, do not compound problems by trying to fix them yourself. Seek help early and fast.

Now, I am in a different marriage, and I'm not just happy, but I feel simply contented and an inexpressible joy as I serve the Lord. I attend church regularly, and I'm plugged into a great Bible study with supportive ladies who help whenever there is a need. I give back through prison ministry, sharing my story and encouraging prisoners to live and lead productive lives, not only when they get out of prison, but whilst they are inside. I encourage them to prepare themselves spiritually, physically and mentally so that they can thrive and re-enter society in a positive role and a firm standing.

My goal is to bring about change by aligning role models to prisoners in a sort of sponsorship relationship, wherein prisoners can successfully learn new coping mechanisms, grow and become productive citizens. Idleness leads to self-destruction and doesn't promote growth. No one should be stagnant – we should all continue learning, setting goals, dreaming dreams and achieving them, no matter where we are in life.

LIFE

Oh, what a life! Sometimes it is full of emptiness,
Sometimes it is full of zest.
But count your blessings, for it could be less.
Some reap the benefits of the harvest they sow,
And others pay the price, but they really don't know.
Labour is tedious and sweat rolls off their brows.
The goods produced are fantastic –
so, why are the prices unrealistic?
Times are much harder, but places and people change – God
never changes.
Economies may be different, but life moves on.
For without toiling, interests or hobbies,
How can we survive?
There are many challenges, privileges and opportunities
Life is a gateway, explore it – it is a wonderful journey!

CHAPTER 15

DEATH

I recall my first experience with grief when my dear friend Jay mourned the loss of his older sister Susy. She had gotten hit by a car by the junction roundabout at Hurley's supermarket. It was such a sad day for my friend and for all of us in grade school who saw him so hurt. He sat with a few of us at the back of the school for a very long time.

One night when I was in prison, I was in maximum security and feeling so sick – I needed to see a doctor. However, the officers completely ignored me. I called several times for help, but no one came. That night, I was so discouraged, despondent and simply wanted to give up. This could have been a night when I tried to end my life. Although I was bipolar for so long, I had never experienced suicidal thoughts because I had a great hope that I carried with me through life. However, this particular night, with all that was happening in my life – prison and my health situation – I simply wanted to end everything. I felt my plate was full and that I couldn't go on anymore. However, I had time to think and drew my attention back to God and my family. This gave me the determination to live.

One day, I met a man named Pastor Nyack, who was presiding over a funeral for a dear but wily gentleman who had been an inspiration in my youth. I had heard my mother talking expressively about Pastor Nyack, saying, "Now, that's my man," as she always referred to pastors who delivered a "tell-it-like-it-is" sermon. The funeral was a wonderfully orchestrated and brief service. The deceased had reached 92 years of age and had lived an esteemed life, particularly within the community amongst his family, neighbours and friends. He was respected and revered.

Pastor Nyack's edict was concise, relevant, effective and well received by all who attended. It was an inspiration! It was healing! It was visionary, and it was purpose-driven!

As I sat and listened, I began to think about death and its representation further. Many people question why, for lack of understanding. We all know that death is inevitable. It comes to us at any point in time. Some people know when death is near, and there are some who don't. As I pondered, God revealed to me that death has swallowed sin, whether directly (natural cause) or indirectly (accidentally).

Physically, death has swallowed sin because of humankind's lack. God foreknew that the world would suffer. However, supernaturally, this same death that swallows sin becomes life more abundantly so that those in Christ will live to reap the benefits of God's grace, power and knowledge.

At this funeral in 2010, I learned the true concept of death. This was so powerful!

I thought about how people need to choose and decide which kind of death they want. In other words, whether they wish to die plainly in sin or whether they want to die to reach eternal life. It's not just about what people say after people have departed, which is always lovely. The question is, have they prepared themselves by living according to God's purpose so that they may deal with death willingly and gain a better perspective of its true design?

After the funeral that opened my eyes, I received a phone call: a long-time friend had come to my house unexpectedly to visit me that very night! I talked to this friend regularly, but our visits were few and far between. I was just leaving the service when I received the telephone call that she was at my house. I was pleasantly surprised for several reasons, but mostly because she was there. What she didn't know was why it took me a while to get home, for she thought it would have been over sooner rather than later. I told her that the funeral was indeed brief, but the graveside service took a long time because it was simply a beautiful burial. Pastor Nyack had a captive audience and particularly engaged a handful of men who were moved and inspired by his message from God. He told us how we must change and live to please God rather than men before it is too late. It was a deliverance, one in which I believed a few were renewed, revived and saved.

Questions:
1. When did you become aware of death?
2. Have you ever envisioned dying?
3. Do you believe you are prepared for eternal life?
4. What was your first experience of death?
5. What did your experience feel like?
6. Are you afraid to die?

RECOVERY AND TRIUMPH

CHAPTER 16

BAPTISM

Although my circumstances pushed me off my intended path, I did return full time to my first love and to church, dedicating my life to the Lord and enjoying my second marriage. Our relationship, of course, is not perfect, but it keeps me happy and on my toes.

I decided that I would settle at First Baptist Church of Grand Cayman, where I met many sisters and brothers in Christ. To this very day, if you ask me why I became a Baptist, I will say because the word Baptist, by nature, is an outward expression of life with Christ in God. I noted that, although some persons do not believe that baptism is essential, it is a very important part of a Christian's life as Christ Himself was baptized into His Father's Kingdom. He, the Father and the Holy Spirit are one, thereby creating the Trinity. Just as each person is a whole – a baby, child and adult – so it is with God, Christ and the Holy Spirit, who live in each one of us. Those who genuinely accept and follow the Trinity are accepted into God's Kingdom. Those who do not are accepting the devil's scheme and his way of life, which leads to perdition. The Word in 1 John 3:10 declares that there are children of God and children of the devil. The two are in constant conflict with each other. I believe that the greater good that lives in us is the Holy Spirit, which wills people to do good. For those who do bad or evil deeds and continue doing so, there are no more sacrifices for their sins. Hebrews 10:26 says, "If we deliberately keep on sinning after we have received the knowledge of the truth, no sacrifice for sins is left." Some people believe they can wait until they are older or nearly dying before giving their lives to God, but they are mistaken. God still sits on His throne, judging His world, and His wrath is very real. Some people claim that nature is responsible for natural disasters, global pandemics, etc. However, I believe that God is echoing His warnings through thunder and lightning and everything in between. The rains are His blessings on His people.

For the second time in my life, I recommitted myself to the Lord. This time, as an adult, I received Baptism in 2007 at Smith's Cove through Cayman Islands Baptist Church (CIBC), although shortly thereafter I returned to First Baptist Church of Grand Cayman, Cayman Islands.

I was baptized in June 2007 by Pastor Mills of CIBC. It was a lovely day, a bit overcast with a little wind. A few close friends, some family members and other members of the church attended. I felt a strong urge that this was the direction in which the Lord had pointed me, so I felt great going under – submersion. I had already conceded that my past life was over, and I vowed to begin a new journey.

I was enjoying my newfound life, attending church and Bible study regularly.

TEMPTATION

I met a man in December 2007 on a Saturday night. I was introduced to him by a married couple; the wife was a practising Christian. I remember the day clearly, as it was the ladies' annual tea party, hosted in the home of Mrs. Oakley from CIBC. It was a beautiful day! My aunt Doll helped, along with some of the other ladies from church. The tables were beautifully arranged and set up with delicate tea pottery and an array of delicacies made by Mrs. Oakley and Mrs. McFadin. I was so delighted to be part of this wonderful gathering, enjoying light conversation and interacting with everyone present. The temperature was great, the conversation flowed, and everything happened naturally.

Later that evening, I left elated, but I returned to my empty five-bedroom house and instantly felt alone. Then, it happened! I was not quite fulfilled with being alone, so I decided to call the wife of a friend to find out what was happening. The conversation basically went something like this. I said, "Hi, how are you, and what are you up to?" I relayed the earlier event. She asked, "Would you like to go to my husband Core's office Christmas party?" I immediately said yes. She said, "Good, we will pick you up shortly." I did not even change my clothes but remained the way I was, dressed in a white rayon blouse and a long, flowing, black-and-white sarong skirt.

The car arrived on cue! My friend came to the door to receive me. She was accompanied by her husband and two passengers, one of whom was named Luis. He immediately got out of the car and opened the door whilst introductions were being made. I took my place in the back seat, smack-dab in the middle of Luis and the other passenger. On our journey to Margaritaville, my friend, her husband and I struck up a conversation whilst the other passengers remained silent.

Margaritaville is a Jimmy Buffett-inspired diner, set upstairs in the old Anchorage building, right in the heart of George Town. The music and decor brought back short-lived memories from my past. The party was in full swing! All five of us walked out onto the veranda. It was a beautiful night overlooking the Hog Sty Bay. The waitress came up, we ordered drinks, and I tried to communicate over the din of the party. Luis sat next to me. The conversation between Luis and I felt natural; he talked and I listened as we completely ignored our other companions.

Growing up, I'd always had a knack for languages, with Spanish being my main focus. That didn't mean I had an exclusive desire for intimate relationships with Spanish men. And yet, the camaraderie between Luis and I was a seduction! The lights dimmed, and he and I danced the night away to the band playing hits from the past. Both of us were seasoned dancers who instantly gelled together.

This relationship took off and lasted for three years. I did not stop going to church during that time. And, although I was besotted with this young man, I was determined not to be a puppet for any man, so I ended the relationship.

CHAPTER 17

BIBLE STUDY

During my incarceration, various churches visited the prison on a weekly basis. I specifically recall Pastor Lang and his group, as well as a group of ladies from the First Baptist Church of Grand Cayman (First Baptist). They were supportive and encouraging. Even though I had messed up, they were there to bring a message of hope.

When the prison warden called church, I felt excited to go – even while locked up, church liberated me. Little did I know that there would be ladies attending who I knew. I was embarrassed, but at the same time happy to see them, as I felt the love emanating from them. The late Mrs. Virginia Castillo, Mrs. Sharon Williams, Mrs. Bev Chin Sinn, Ms. Dawn Budal and Ms. Nicky Johnson were all there praising God, even for a prisoner like me.

What gave me strength during this, the most difficult period in my life, was when Nicky sent me a letter emphasizing God's love for me. Dawn sent me her tattered, cherished Bible, which I was eager to explore. This is one way that others can help people that are not only incarcerated, but otherwise going through difficult times such as depression, anxiety and loneliness.

Upon my release, the late Mrs. Virginia invited me to lunch and to return to church. I immediately accepted. Lunch was lovely at Legendz, a diner. She told me how Christ loved me unconditionally, so much so that he died to take away my sins. This led me to return to church, where I was eager to attend each Sunday. Before incarceration, I had wandered from church to church. However, because of the love and support shown from the church group, I decided that I would become a member of First Baptist.

Once I became a member, Ms. Marie Ebanks-Blake invited me to attend a home group Bible study led by Ms. Dawn. I hesitated at first but said I would check it out. After some time, I decided to attend the Bible study home group. I met a bunch of lovely ladies who were all welcoming. Only a few of them knew my story at that time. Studying the Bible together became exciting, and I had a yearning to return each week. Attending Bible study and resuming attendance at Church became the norm for me. I faithfully attended and took every opportunity to be at church. If you do the same, you will find that your feelings of inadequacy diminish as time moves on. You will feel revived and renewed.

Having these ladies in my life gave me an opportunity to really see that I was not rejected or resented for having bipolar or committing a crime. Some of them knew me personally and knew me before my time in prison, and even before my diagnosis.

I am so grateful for the times we have spent together as sisters in Christ. To this day, we are still in touch. I would highly recommend anyone to see how Bible study can be helpful and just how important it is for Christians to hold a person's hands, not only when they are on top of the mountain, but also during the hard times when they are in the valley. Times like these really highlight what Christianity is all about.

Church and Bible study are helpful because we are all supposed to be on the same page with no judgements. We should show acceptance and brotherly love to glorify God. This way of life will essentially help you overcome struggles and allow you to deal with life's complexities level-headedly. Serving God has changed my life, and I am joyful even when there is turmoil and chaos around me. A good cure for mood swings is constantly training your mind to think Godly thoughts rather than relying on yourself. This is why the Bible plays a big part in how to live and how to have healthy relationships and thoughts.

God has a place for you and can change your life. Seek him, and He will do more than you could ever ask for.

Questions:

1. Do you have questions about the Bible?
2. Do you want to know more about the Bible and who Jesus is?
3. Would you like to know what Jesus can do for you?
4. Do you think attending Bible Study is important?
5. Would you attend a Bible Study home group?
6. How do you think church and Bible Study can help you?
7. Are you afraid of feeling inadequate or silly at Bible Study?
8. Are you ashamed of knowing nothing about Christ?

CHAPTER 18

A LEADER AND A SERVANT

RESPONSIBILITIES, WELFARE AND VOLUNTARY WORK
Church and family life became my focus. I had the responsibility of maintaining a mortgaged house, which I could simply not afford. One of my sisters and my brother-in-law helped me with monthly payments, just so I had a roof over my head and so I would not lose my house. First Baptist Church of Grand Cayman, the church I attended, assisted me as well.

I helped the church on a regular basis by filling the pews with informational pamphlets and visitors' cards. I enjoyed doing this for the time. One of my brothers assisted too. I also received food vouchers from the Department of Social Services. Life as I knew it had drastically changed and got harder, but with God, I knew that nothing was impossible.

I prayed fervently. I would say, "Lord, if you want me to keep this house or lose it, either way, I submit it all to you. Have your way, Lord." With that, I surrendered.

At the same time, I had a yearning to genuinely help other prisoners, particularly recidivists who had difficulties staying out of prison. I began prison ministry in 2012, accompanying Ms. Cathy Gomez, the prison chaplain, on a weekly basis. I went to the men's prison on Sunday evenings and the women's prison on Tuesday mornings. Oh, how I loved visiting the prisons, for I knew that there were good and even some innocent people in both places.

I enjoyed the many Sunday evenings spent driving to the men's prison with Cathy, Pastor Alson Ebanks and Edward Solomon. We merrily chatted and sang songs – a wonderful experience. Sunday nights, on the way back from the prison, we had dessert fellowship at my house.

I enjoyed helping so much so that I was invited to join the board of Prison Fellowship Cayman, where I became the Angel Tree coordinator. The Angel Tree is a programme through which participating churches purchase gifts on behalf of incarcerated parents, and either deliver them to kids or send them to the prison for the parents to give to their children when they visit. This also affords church congregations the opportunity to talk to families about Christ and perhaps invite them to church. It was and is a very exciting way to help. I am responsible for coordinating various churches, tallying the gifts, sorting them out and organizing the delivery process. I continue to work closely with the prison chaplain, who is Pastor Bentley Robinson at the time of writing this book.

I wrote the following in my diary when I began prison ministry:

HER MAJESTY'S PRISON
HMP NORTHWARD – MEN'S PRISON

Sunday, 19 August 2012

DAY 1

I received a call from Ms. Gomez earlier in the week, notifying me that I had received approval to visit the prisons, supervised by her or Pastor Bentley Robinson of First Baptist Church.

I was elated, as it had been four years since I had written to the Director of Prisons and had not received a response. I was so passionate about helping other prisoners that I did not give up. Ms. Gomez collected me around 6:10pm. We drove 15 minutes to Northward Prison, which houses male inmates. a men's correctional facility. During the drive, we struck up several interesting conversations.

Upon arrival, there were two other female visitors waiting in the parking lot. Then, five others appeared, including an ex-prisoner.

As we entered the main gate, the click of the first gate brought back memories, particularly of the night of Hurricane Ivan, as this was where all the female prisoners sheltered during that dreadful time. We cleared the first and second gates. Then, we had to walk through a scanner and proceed through another four gates.

The entrance reeked of animal urine, as there were animals living on the other side of the prison fence: cows, chickens and birds. As we walked through the final gate, we spotted one or two prisoners. Their faces lit up!

Our group was on our way to the chapel to minister to the prisoners. The chapel was quite large and in an upstairs building. Ms. Ethel and I greeted the men as they came in one by one. One of the first prisoners who came into the chapel was a fellow who I recognized.

I was immediately taken aback – the equal amount of astonishment on his face made it obvious that something was wrong. As far as I knew, this man had died a long time ago in a freak accident in which a boat had capsized, killing one person. I said his name. He said, "Yes, this is me." Apparently, shortly after the incident, he had left the Island. He was gone for several years before being extradited back to Cayman.

Ms. Gomez, a skilled organist, and a prisoner, who was also a drummer, began playing the music. Then, Ed Solomon and Mrs. Linda started to lead the singing. "Wow, what a beautiful praise and worship," I thought to myself. I really felt God in this place as my heart felt overwhelmed with emotion.

After a few songs, a prayer opened the fellowship. All of us were excited, as the ex-prisoner would share his testimony this evening. However, the ex-prisoner gave us a sermon! He had been released a year prior and turned his life around, and he was doing really well. It was a joy to see him stand at the podium, take the microphone and just preach without any notes. The group was impressed, but at the same time, I knew they would love to hear his testimony. His sermon was based on Matthew 20:22, about the withered fig tree. He reminded the men that no matter how big their problems were, they could overcome them.

After the sermon and closing song, the ex-prisoner called the prison men forward, those who really wanted to change their lives. He prayed for them and gave them each a tract. Prison ministry finished by 8 o'clock, but of course, before we left, the men were eager to start conversations. However, we had to leave.

The prison officer was there to receive us. It was an awesome experience!

***

Tuesday, 21 August 2012

HMP FAIRBANKS – WOMEN'S PRISON

I agreed to meet Ms. Gomez this morning at 8:30am at HMP Fairbanks, a prison for women. I arrived right on time, and Ms. Gomez awaited my arrival; together, we proceeded to enter the prison.

Ms. Gomez buzzed in. An officer who I recognized came forward to open the main gate. She and I were both excited. Although it felt strange to me, we agreed that I was visiting under different circumstances – that is, as a visitor.

Walking in again and hearing the jingling of the keys and the click of the padlock, I experienced a tingly feeling. The prison looked more or less the same, although it had a few tiny changes. Another officer was in the office. She too was happy to see me doing so well.

Ms. Gomez and I handed in our keys and any cell phones that were in our possession. Ms. Gomez went to enquire about a female prisoner who she wanted to see. I then struck up conversation with the two officers, filling them in on what I had been up to.

There were only three female prisoners in the entire prison. Ms. Gomez had gone through the door to see the young lady she had enquired about. Whilst I awaited her return, a female prisoner came forward to say that she was the only one coming out today for fellowship.

One of the officers then ushered me in, along with the prisoner, to begin our visit. I was happy to have a few moments with her. As we began our conversation, I discovered that she was a very impressive young lady.

Before we met, she had been busy cleaning and working outside, but she had to come back inside because it started to rain. I introduced myself, and we made light conversation. I did not ask why she was there, but instead asked about her job there, how she spent her time, about her family, etc.

Ms. Gomez then entered. She got right into ministry, reading a passage of scripture that related to events that had unfolded in both the prisoner and Ms. Gomez's weeks. She prayed for the worship and used the Elmslie Memorial Hymnal. I was overjoyed, as hearing a hymn that I had not heard or sang for a long time brought back memories of how I used to sing. The lady prisoner's week had been very busy, and she told us all about what her responsibilities were. I sat and listened and chimed in every now and then. However, when Ms. Gomez asked me to share a few words, I was a bit nervous, but at the same time, I felt wonderfully surprised, as it was on my first day visiting with her, and I thought I was just going to watch and listen. Without much fuss, I began to share advice about how one can pass time and gave a bit of encouragement, too...

We spent two hours there before we left. Ms. Gomez and I retrieved our belongings. An officer came forward to let us out. Outside the gate, Ms. Gomez asked if I would be back next week. I quickly said I had to work out my schedule, but I thought I would be. This was the start of my first prison ministry experience.

This visit was different to my trip to the men's prison because there we went to the chapel for praise and worship, while at HMP Fairbanks we had a one-on-one session with a prisoner. The latter was the experience that I wanted to have, as I would like to be able to reach out to prisoners on an individual basis to bring about successful change in that prisoner's life.

***

Going to visit the prisons gave me an opportunity to lead. I led the singing whilst Ms. Gomez played the organ. There was also room for sharing or giving testimonies. The time flew by so quickly with every visit as we began and ended with either a prayer or our favourite theme song, "For Those Tears I Died".

A DAUGHTER'S PLEA TO HER FATHER

A father is supposed to understand,
Not only to command!
A daughter's pain he does not know,
Only when she tells him so!
He's there to comfort and to share,
The burdens of life's journeys,
That are hard to bear.
Listen, Papa, I demand!
I would really like you to understand!
I am not submissive to destruction,
Only to life's journeys and that's from instruction.
Help me to help myself so well,
That all around me can tell.
To be pill laden is not what God intended.
Otherwise, He would not have descended!
Yes, doctors are there, I agree!
But not to stifle you unhealthily!
Their opinion is to share,
Not to give you more pain than you can bear.
I am assertive and that's no lie!
Help me daily just to get by.
Times are changing – tales are long!
Let me remain stable and strong.
Do not cripple my ability – I am sane!
Let me not wane.
You've taught me the value of independence – that's a plus!
Now I should live my life, and that's a must!
A father's there to guide you to adulthood,
Not to criticize behaviour that's good!
I'm your daughter who tells you the truth,
Even though certain points are moot!
Thank you for being there when you could.
I love you and that's no shroud!

So, walk beside me, Papa,
Hold my hand – I'm a woman now,
So please understand.
I can make decisions about my life.
I'm your grown daughter, not your wife!
So, I must go on being me!
Happy, healthy and free,
The person God created me to be.

God bless you, Papa!

CHAPTER 19

EFFECTS OF PRISON AND BIPOLAR: SOCIALLY, OCCUPATIONALLY AND EMOTIONALLY

SOCIALLY

Although I never anticipated it, anyone can end up in prison. Prison for me was a period of guilt and shame, but also rest and restoration. I felt guilt and shame because I committed a crime and was locked away from a world I once knew. On the other hand, I could also rest because I had been burning the candle at both ends while dealing with a divorce, the loss of my children, broken relationships, loneliness and committing a crime. God has a way of grabbing our attention. And then, even when we are in the mud, he has a way of making us clean. He fully drew me back to himself and restored my life. I had no choice but to cling to the one I knew for certain would be able to help me.

Some of the fears I had were rejection, others' resentment and my own loneliness. However, upon my release, I had support from some family members, and the church and some friends never gave up on me.

I recall that, on the day I was released, my mama had a surprise welcome home gathering for me. I was stunned by this and, at the same time, cowered because of shame and thought I would be bombarded with questions. So, I excused myself from the party and went back into isolation at my mama's house.

Fear gripped me because I did not know how to start over. However, God guided me throughout my imprisonment, preparing me to set myself up spiritually, mentally and physically. I did not waste time during incarceration or after.

I presumed I would get backlash from people in my community. If I did, I never experienced it face to face. If that were to happen, because of God's love and mercy, I would know how to respond. I also believe that people spared their judgment because I was known for my good character before incarceration, which I quickly reclaimed after prison.

The goal is to find people who genuinely wish to help, and I felt loved by those who pursued my friendship. I am grateful to each one of them.

OCCUPATIONALLY

People who go to prison are often rejected, resented, mistrusted and misguided. Society can be cruel and prejudiced, as well as unforgiving. However, undaunted, I was determined not to let anyone keep me down.

I had written two business plans whilst incarcerated and had prayed about securing a job in property maintenance. One plan was a bed and breakfast; the other was a halfway house built especially for prisoners who wanted to reclaim their lives.

Upon release, I saw an advert in the newspaper regarding an opening for an office manager at a property management company. I applied and, during my interview, shared my story honestly. I was given the job on the spot.

However, the job only went well for a bit before I succumbed to an episode of bipolar. My boss was very sympathetic, but I felt at a loss because of where I'd been, how I was perceived as a prisoner, whether I would be trusted, and how struggling with bipolar made me feel. My boss was kind and considerate, as well as compassionate. She had given me a chance, and I served her well.

I soon recovered from the episode but had a most difficult time returning to work and coping with my re-birth after bipolar. I say re-birth because, every time I go through episodes, I must literally learn how to live again, how to concentrate and how to socialize. Again, God has been beside me all the way, and in moments such as these, I revert to Him.

This time around, I had difficulties finding another job that paid well or in which I was qualified and experienced. Everyone wanted to see a police record, and I was not willing to produce one because of my guilt, shame and embarrassment. I was struggling – but I was not deterred!

So, I resumed my activities and did truly feel interested in working again. I decided that I would pursue opening the bed and breakfast. I did do short-term rentals for a period, but because I had mortgaged a property, I was forced to do long-term rentals for financial stability. To this very day, I am still taking long-term tenancies and enjoying meeting new people from different walks of life. God has been so good to me.

I thought I would never be able to secure employment in the legal field again. However, I received a job offer from a small law firm seeking an office manager. I was elated, as this gentleman and lady were quite sharp in the areas of law, and I was back working in my field.

I want to encourage anyone – not just those suffering from a mental condition or dealing with a prison sentence – to not give up on themselves. If God has forgiven you, who are others to judge you? If you seek God, he will open doors for you. Stand firm in your Christian beliefs, and it will deter you from making the same mistake I did.

EMOTIONALLY

I was literally spent, drained and despondent. Going to prison took its toll on me, but the good news was that I never stayed there. God was with me all the way. I was soothed, loved and cared for by Him. Once you accept this knowledge, he will carry you through anything, even in the direst circumstances.

I resented some family members at times because they thought they knew best, but they only stepped in when I was already in the valley. Some wanted to make decisions as to what should happen. The help was often rejected, as they sought medical intervention for me rather than inquiring about what was really happening in my life at the time. Sometimes when this happened, I was pushed into the hands of professionals, who I felt circumvented the problems and instead made them more complicated by administering drugs that were not necessary at that moment. I felt they did not really see me for who I was. This was truly tiring and frustrating – it is like putting a band-aid on someone's problems.

Having bipolar can leave you drained and somewhat robbed of a life. However, the greatest thing I have is God as my refuge and strength. He is an ever-present help in times of trouble, as written in Psalm 46:1. Relying on God really keeps me centred in this life.

Some people do not understand the depth of pain, anguish, depression and suppression that one with a mental condition goes through. Everybody has issues at some point in their lives; however those who have extra challenges can be so distraught without God.

I presume family members have a hard time for many reasons, too. Some do not take the time, or they are hurting or busy, or they try but lack understanding. I am aware that it is a difficult situation for families to cope with, as they might not know what to do and wish the problem would go away. It is painful for the family to see their loved one suffering from a mental condition, committing a crime and going to prison too. I must reiterate that there was no correlation between me having bipolar and committing a crime. The divorce, separation from my children and my feeling of brokenness were heart-piercing and harsh, and out of these feelings sprung shock, bitterness and resentment. This was not an excuse, but a fact.

Most times in my family, I feel unheard, rejected and ignored. However, I have learned and am still learning how to cope with my circumstances. At family gatherings, there were periods when I felt silent stigmatism against me. I felt alone, like an outcast. It seemed that no one cared to take the time to understand how badly broken I was. Everything was veneered and not dealt with at the level that I needed.

Many years later, my extended family still does not discuss my bipolar, but they do understand that I have come a long way and am living the best life I can. Regardless, life is certainly better with my family in it.

During my last episode of bipolar, I was hospitalized. I became attached to Mr. Hugh Chin Sinn, a brother from First Baptist, who helped me tremendously. He was by my bedside night and day for the entire three weeks. I will never forget his kindness expressed in love and action. I thank God for my husband Rubén, who was always beside me, and Ms. Cathy Gómez for her wise counsel. The Christianly love shown was well received – I thrived on it. This kindness affected me so much that my recovery was much shorter and healthier. There were other kindnesses extended to me. It was very helpful for me. God was certainly taking care of my needs.

If you find people who understand you and your personality, engage with and relate to them. You will find that they genuinely want to get to know you for who you are. Pray for others who are not so readily willing and move on. God has many creatures.

CHAPTER 20

AN INMATE'S PERSPECTIVE

All of us have been nurtured as children in some way or another; even if we were neglected, someone had to help us reach where we are today. Regardless of our circumstances, most of us still manage to find our way home, although there are those who will remain wayward if they never gain any perspective.

Think back to when you were a child and how lovingly someone cared for you. For example, when you were hungry, they fed you; when you needed a new diaper, they changed you; and when you cried, they soothed you. These were necessary steps that propelled you forward. You had to learn to crawl before you could walk. Pause for a moment – have you ever wondered how you got to the point where you could walk? Who helped you? Yes, one or both parents, your sister or brother, or another relative may have guided you. But think again – who ultimately helped you? The spirit of God that dwells within you gave you the will to get there.

As you grew from an infant to a toddler, then went on to preschool, I would like you to focus on who the key players were: God, then your parents, siblings, extended family and the environment. Pause again, and now think about and picture your preschool to high school years. Look at the key players: friends, the environment, teachers, family, God. Do you notice how the players changed and the order in which they appear?

Those who have or haven't made it through to high school; or those who have gone to college, university or the workforce; or those who have gone on a wayward path: think about and picture the key players at this stage in your lives and the order in which they appeared. You may see friends, money, career, education, welfare, waywardness, family, God… Pause. Have you noticed anything? Have you seen the way the key players have once again been considerably rearranged?

Now that you have vividly captured this image in your mind, do you see a pattern, a process or a method, or do you see a messed-up picture?

What can be seen from the above pattern is that, for many of us, God has been placed last in our thoughts and actions or perhaps has consistently been left out of our lives altogether. To be successful, you must return to the basics. Learn from the source that motivated you to strive for milestones, to strive for independence – and to strive for life in general.

Whether the key players in your circumstances were negative or positive doesn't matter. What matters is God's intention for your life. We have our parents' nurturing and our will to spur us forward, but because the spirit of God is placed within each of us, God is the one responsible for successful change. His very foundation provided you with substance to help you grow. It provided you with sustenance to keep you focused. It gave you the abilities and tools to propel you forward and help you live and lead a productive life. This foundation was never designed to lead us to a destructive path, but somehow, in the sequence of events in our lives, we get off track. But we can find ourselves in a good place on our return from prison, given:

1. An opportunity;
2. A degree of freedom;
3. A sense of responsibility and accountability;
4. And an observation and a reflection to look into our lives, to explore and examine where we have gone wrong.

In her book *Get Out of That Pit*, Beth Moore wrote, "Whether we put ourselves in a pit, have fallen or have slipped into a pit, we can get out!" In other words, we are not all the same, our circumstances are different, and our stories are unique. Nevertheless, God skilfully crafted our fundamental design from the beginning – and that's true for all of us. There are people willing to help in all the stages of life. You just need to change your focus and gain a new perspective. You need to find your way back. I am being helped. Are you?

I would like you to really think about the following questions – the choice is really yours!

Questions:
1. Have you looked back on your story with the method described above?
2. Have you examined the players in your story and whether they have had a positive or negative effect on your life?
3. Have you considered adjusting or rearranging the players in your story, or have you given up?
4. Are you discouraged and frustrated by the same results?
5. Are you willing to change your circumstances?

HELP IS AVAILABLE, AND IT STARTS WITH YOU!

A GLIMPSE OF HEAVEN

Look around and you will see
a glimpse of Heaven in you and me.
God reveals a grand design
So, sit back and recline.
See how Heaven unfolds
In the lives of those foretold.
The earth on which we live is craven –
Ain't no time for misbehaving.
God is mighty, and He's great!
Subject yourselves and feel elated!
He has provided all our needs
So come on, you and me,
Let us sow some seeds.
Let the beauty of Heaven be seen
Crowned in His Glory, sovereignty realm.
Set the table, come to the feast
A full banquet is His delight, not the least.
Children of God is His victory won
Until Heaven on earth is done.

CHAPTER 21

APPLICATION

There are several key points that are important and can help you when you are going through a crisis.

DO NOT ISOLATE

During my messy divorce, I was lonely but for one dear friend, Vandeen, who lived in another district. I had no financial resources and no family support – I was simply spent. During this time of depressive isolation, I gave way to negative thoughts that got the better of my ego. Don't make decisions based on these feelings of wanting to be alone. Call someone whose intellectual and emotional abilities are stronger than yours.

In other words, when you are going through a crisis, do not isolate. Isolation is when you lock yourself away, spending a lot of time on your own and relying on yourself to get you through. This can be detrimental to your health during a depressive episode. Seek help fast, as depression can be subtle! Self-sufficiency to an extreme extent is destructive. Instead, learn to ask for what is necessary to pull you out of a crisis – whether you have physical, mental, financial or spiritual needs, seek help! Do not rely on yourself. Had I sought Godly counsel during my own depressive episode, I could have overcome the state of loneliness and strengthened my resolve more quickly. The popular cliché, "No man is an island," is so true. So, don't do it alone – reach out!

EXERCISE AND EAT WELL

At a time when your emotional well-being is compromised, your physical well-being can be too, so it's important to try and boost both. Exercise is a key way to reduce stress. In my case, I panicked and became fearful! I wondered how I could survive on my own. If you have thoughts like these, I suggest that you pay attention to your body's needs. Eat, go for a walk and get some fresh air! Exercise, even if it is just for half an hour.

I knew at that point that I couldn't motivate myself enough to spur positive ideas, considering the state I was in. However, looking back, I could have found the energy to go for a simple walk, which would have cleared my mind and propelled me to do something positive with my time.

My counsellor Mike taught me the acronym H.A.L.T., which stands for Hungry, Angry, Lonely and Tired. When I ran on empty, I could not think beyond my problems. So, I know it is very important to apply the key concepts above. H.A.L.T. and eat! By doing so, you will be feeding your brain and getting the strength necessary to sustain you.

When you become angry, acknowledge it and resolve any issues as quickly as possible. Do not stay in a state of anger. My negative thoughts became a central focus and did not help my circumstances. Loneliness and depression, as stated above, can get you into serious problems if they are not quickly addressed. Trying to handle everything by yourself is exhaustive and will lead you to excessive tiredness. Running on empty can and will deplete any resources you have to help you think clearly, so be sure to nourish your body with food.

PRAY AND ACCEPT HELP

Pray and ask for help, and accept it when given to you. Many of us talk ourselves through a crisis rather than speaking to God through prayer. We are not all-sufficient; only God is! Prayer helps us to recognize that we are not alone and that we have someone to help us. Through prayer, God will direct us to interdependency rather than independence by allowing us to connect with people who can and will help us. Had I reached out to my pastor or perhaps my trusted Christian friends, I could have been saved from my dilemma and incarceration.

I encourage anyone going through a crisis, whether you are a Christian or not, to actively pursue help. Do not just accept your dire circumstances or handle them yourself. Reach out!

SET GOALS

Setting goals for oneself is an important, effective and motivating method for time management. It is crucial to set a routine and structure your days to give direction and order to your life. If there is no direction, boredom and idleness will lead to negative thoughts and unproductive actions. Now, I thrive on growth and achievements.

In my opinion, if one is not setting goals for themselves, they become stagnant and lazy as well. Proverbs 13:4 says, "A sluggard's appetite is never filled, but the desires of the diligent are fully satisfied." Therefore, we must not get lazy – we must strive toward something in every area of our lives. God did not put us in this world to simply exist and be unproductive. Colossians 1:10 says, "So as to walk in a manner worthy of the Lord, fully pleasing to him, bearing fruit in every good work and increasing in the knowledge of God."

I often remind my children that the Bible is a blueprint for living. If one were to use the Bible and apply its truths, one would live a better life. Life would certainly not be problem-free, but one would find it easier to cope with life's complexities.

Set some goals and live this life like an overcomer, not an underachiever. It is a journey worth exploring and accomplishing. I wish for everyone to be successful in their pursuits. Believing in God and living to glorify Him is certainly a reason to live, as he offers the hope of eternal life.

CREATE A FLEXIBLE SCHEDULE

Having a flexible schedule helps in terms of giving yourself time to relax throughout the day. Just imagine if I worked a full-time job and suffered from sleep deprivation – I would not be able to function at all. Life for me at this point is balanced, and I am so thankful I have the opportunity to be self-employed. If you cannot make this option work, I would encourage you to seek something that doesn't overwhelm you and stick to it. Whatever you choose, keep growing – do not stagnate.

On the other hand, I also make time to slow myself down by doing things that are not stressful. For example, I take walks, listen to relaxing music or write down my thoughts.

Galatians 5:22–23 says, "The fruits of the Spirit help us to live this life according to God's purpose, for the fruits of the Spirit are love, joy, peace, patience, kindness, goodness, faithfulness, gentleness and self-control, for such there is no law."

Human beings are certainly not perfect. However, if we made a concerted effort to live by the fruits of the Spirit, our lives would be far more gratifying. These fruits include:

LOVE

God is love! Love is a real feeling that is deep-rooted, a fondness or tenderness toward something or someone. It is a feel-good indicator. The opposite of love is not hate, as some people say, but rather indifference. I say this just because if one does not love, this does not mean they hate. Instead, they may be callous or unfeeling toward someone or something. Choosing to love means you share that feeling with others, but also that you are open to receiving love too. It's a much different way of life than one of indifference, as you would experience coldness, rashness, and/or disgruntled feelings instead, thereby creating an atmosphere and exhibiting behaviours that can be very unloving. So, love in action is kindness or good deeds to others.

JOY

God's inexpressible joy is what I longed for, and thankfully I have it now. Regardless of what I have been through, in this phase of my life, I feel joyful and content even if my surroundings are problematic. I am in the state of being filled with joy. The opposite of joy is sadness, a feeling that you can embrace temporarily, but I would not advise you to stay there long. Instead, acknowledge your sad state and eventually move; otherwise, this could lead to long periods of depression and negativity.

PEACE

I would encourage anyone to seek peace, as it surpasses all understanding. Pray and ask God to give you His peace, and you will experience it in every area of your life. Remove unrest, as this is not a feel-good indicator. Instead, it can cause stress as you wrestle with your emotions, and it can and will show up in your actions toward others.

PATIENCE

Patience is something that takes time for many of us to uncover. I am learning as I grow older to slow down and pay attention to how I respond to others in terms of being patient. Whether it is caring for my aged parents, waiting in traffic or trying to hear out others without interjecting, I draw on this fruit of the Spirit. The opposite of patience is intolerance toward a thing or a person, which can lead to anxiety. If one is not careful, removing their shroud of patience can lead to careless mishaps, undesirable results and disappointments. Many of us will, in turn, act curtly toward others when these scenarios play out and patience wears thin.

KINDNESS

Kindness is being thoughtful and considerate to others and to oneself – we must do the latter to succeed in the former. Being kind makes us connect to others in a way that is reciprocal for the most part. A kind word can repel animosity. The opposite of kindness is cruelty to something or someone, and this creates an unpleasant feeling not only toward a person or thing, but toward oneself, too. In other words, cruelty doesn't feel good. It is downright mean to be unkind, particularly if it is unwarranted. Remove the garment of unkindness and put on kindness – you will see a huge difference in yourself and in the those who you treat with care.

GOODNESS

The Bible says no one does good.

As it is written in Romans 3:12, "All have turned away, they have together become worthless; there is no one who does good, not even one."

To display this goodness, we need God – we are not good on our own merit. As human beings, we are often prone to thinking negatively before thinking positively. It is just our sinful nature. So, we must constantly make an effort to train our minds to think good thoughts toward others or toward something. We are always grappling with something, whether it is our perceived inadequacies or our actions toward others. Remove the garment of goodness, and we simply have badness. Who in their right mind wants to wear the garment of badness, which inevitably leads to trouble? This trouble can be in the mind and stem from negative thoughts or experiences, or perhaps from wanting something you shouldn't have. It may also stem from peer pressure.

FAITHFULNESS

Faithfulness means you are consistent in how you do something or treat someone. It is an admirable characteristic. Faithfulness should be worn constantly, as it is unique to be being known as such. We strive for faithfulness but can only achieve it with God's grace. As human beings, we sometimes have the tendency to give up rather than continue our pursuit of faithfulness. Some of us fall short when we give up on things that are good for us to appease someone or to do something else. For example, we might not go to church, or we might give up on a hobby to do another one instead. Remove faithfulness, and you will get unfaithfulness or unreliability. This is not a good thing because there is a lack of trust or a feeling of disloyalty in someone who isn't faithful. So, try wearing the garment of faithfulness regularly, which can lead you to be faithful in every area of your life.

GENTLENESS

Gentleness is a learned behavior that can be difficult to embody in certain situations. For example, we may be gentle to outsiders, but not so mellow toward our families in a similar scenario. Gentleness often gives way to a calmness that is displayed in actions toward others, and your softness lets them appreciate being tender too. The opposite of gentleness is harshness, or being very rough and unkind. These traits are often unyielding and can be led to coldness and insensitivity. So, try being gentle to display the kindness and calmness that you and others need.

SELF-CONTROL

God gives each one of us the ability to have self-control with His instructive purpose. Self-control is to be exercised in every area of our lives – being mindful of overindulgence in any particular thing or situation. For example, we are called to have self-control with our emotions and in our actions. Without God, this is impossible. With God in our lives, all things are possible because he gives us the strength to resist the devil's schemes. One can ultimately have self-control in the way we are taught, as we instinctively know right from wrong. As innate beings, we feel when things are bad for us or when they are right. We lack self-control when we do things that we want because they make us feel good, even though we know they might be wrong. Self-control takes a lot of work and effort; for example, overcoming destructive habits such as overindulgence, drunkenness, extramarital affairs and so forth. God knows we are not perfect beings – that is why Jesus came to deliver us from our sins and redeem us so that we could have eternal life. Remove the garment of self-control, and what do you get? Chaos, dysfunction and disorder.

If everyone embodied the fruits of the Spirit, there would be no reason to have laws – everyone would be abiding and living accordingly. But this can only be achieved with the help of the good Lord. So, keep on striving as the fruits of the Spirit are always a work in progress.

That greater good that lives in each one of us compels us to do good things, and I believe that is God's will. The evil that resides in each one of us is of the devil, and we can only overcome by choosing to embody the greater good that lives within us instead. For example, our thoughts are generally negative before they become positive. We must constantly pray to God to overcome them. Some of those thoughts can be very subtle. For example, "I hate her," or, "I don't like him." We can reverse those same thoughts by God's grace, and only His grace. Human beings are prone to fail without God.

LONGING
Written after my imprisonment

Like a mate waiting for the ship to dock
with a much-desired longing,
the anticipation, the climax,
and heartache eagerly cascading,
searching for that frantic soul.
A love long lost to years of
starvation and deprivation.
The weight of shackles
restraining one desperately seeking
to relinquish the bondage to explore
and discover a world that was filled
with love, structure and oneness
where family speaks volumes.
The strength of a woman is
shown in her weakness;
the ability to hope, to overcome,
and to navigate a journey so powerful
only God can fathom.
The intermittent attributes that
display permanence in a world
desperately seeking to destroy,
but for God's reassurance time after time.
The brutality, the indifference
that signifies man's demise.
Only God can rescue from devastation,
disreputability and void.
The heart of the soul bleeds
as negative energy cruises
through the arteries seeking to devour,
to quench its thirst,
as God grasps the soul
and nurses it back to the state of being

in accord with his oneness
and awe-inspired fused energy
that emanates an abundance
of positive, regenerative deliverance.
"Loneliness" is an appeasement of
separation from God's universe
into a world of nothingness,
but to be "alone" is to be in God's presence,
His grace communing with all of
nature's wonder as only He intended.
His hands are forever outstretched,
never ceasing, but always comforting,
strengthening and fine-tuning.
It is with this knowledge that
souls are rescued from the conundrum
of society's aloofness
into a world of symphony,
orchestrated by the Master's hands.
In a world of the unknown,
we travel by faith.

AFTERWORD

SPONSOR A PRISONER FOUNDATION (SPF)

Crime should not be encouraged. However, once a crime has been committed, the government is largely responsible for funding inmates. This funding is very basic, and the inmate is often without the full care and attention they need, in terms of personal assistance.

The inmate has already incurred due punishment by being locked away from society and denied normal privileges. It is not at all beneficial to society if many of these inmates continue to be repeat offenders, thereby being a further nuisance to society.

To reduce the rate of recidivism, I would like to establish what I call the Sponsor a Prisoner Foundation (SPF), which will provide prisoners with necessities, such as regular contact with family and friends, care packages, proper care and a role model from the community to be there throughout each person's sentence. All of this will equip them for a better life – and encourage them to stay out of prison.

SPF will ensure that the inmate receives care packages monthly and has regular weekly visits from their sponsor, so that they can establish a good rapport with each other.

An inmate will be sponsored only once in their lifetime. It would not be an aim to continue sponsoring inmates if they have already been helped through this foundation. SPF will instead give that chance to another inmate who genuinely wants to change their lifestyle. It will also look as if the foundation is catering to inmates who continue to commit crimes. The foundation will support inmates who:

1. Show remorse, and
2. Would like to be a part of the solution, rather than to continue being a problem to society.

The foundation will, in turn:

1. Prepare them to face tough situations upon re-entering society
2. Encourage them to choose better companions, and
3. Help inmates to move on and establish a better life.

I envision SPF as a voluntary, non-profit organization that leads inmates to a crime-free life, thus decreasing the rate of recidivism. This foundation would be open to monetary donations and to volunteers who are committed to help make a difference in an inmate's life.

> Those interested in helping make SPF a reality may write to the author at:
> PO Box 1009, Grand Cayman KY1-1102.

ACKNOWLEDGEMENTS

This book has been a long time coming. I could not seem to piece it all together, but I just knew that God had prepared me along the way. Thanks to God – it was simply impossible for me to write this book without Him. All the pieces I had written over time came together beautifully.

I could not have embarked on such a project if it had not been for key people in my life. I wish to acknowledge Mike Chester, whose sincere approach to counselling made it quite an easy way of expressing myself. Thanks to my brother Rex Ebanks for encouraging me to write my story. Praises to Sandra Miller for sticking it out, even when there were ugly times. She completely understood! Thanks to my family and friends, especially Luis Quiñonez, who had the patience to put up with me, and my dear friend Core Fatels for always getting back on track with me. Thanks to my church family! Special thanks to Roy and Nancy Bodden for reading the manuscript and believing in my potential to get the book published. And thanks to Dr. Erica Gordon and Cathy Gomez for editing my book. I could not have done it without their input and wise advice.

Thanks to Dr. Lacey, who got it right – she was the breakthrough doctor! I am grateful for her wise counsel, although I was not always pleased. A big thank you to the mental health nurses, some of whom genuinely cared.

And finally, thank you to my husband Rubén Lopez Monzon for the love, support and patience to stay up during corrections.

God bless you all for the support and love shown.

ABOUT CHERISH EDITIONS

Cherish Editions is a bespoke author-funded publishing service for mental health, well-being and inspirational books.

As a division of the TriggerHub Group, the UK's leading independent mental health and well-being organization, we are experienced in creating and selling positive, responsible, important and inspirational pieces of bibliotherapy. Our books harness the power of a person's lived experience to guide others through their own mental health journeys and kick-start their recovery. We also work to de-stigmatize the issues around mental health and improve the well-being of those who read our titles.

Founded by Adam Shaw, a mental health advocate, author and philanthropist, and leading psychologist Lauren Callaghan, Cherish Editions aims to publish books that provide advice, support and inspiration. We nurture our authors so that their stories can unfurl on the page, helping them to share their uplifting and moving stories.

Cherish Editions is unique in that a percentage of the profits from the sale of our books goes directly to leading mental health charity Shawmind, to deliver its vision to provide support for those experiencing mental ill health.

Find out more about Cherish Editions by visiting cherisheditions.com or by joining us on:
  Twitter @cherisheditions
  Facebook @cherisheditions
  Instagram @cherisheditions

Cherish
EDITIONS

ABOUT SHAWMIND

A proportion of profits from the sale of all Trigger books go to their sister charity, Shawmind, also founded by Adam Shaw and Lauren Callaghan. The charity aims to ensure that everyone has access to mental health resources whenever they need them.

You can find out more about the work Shawmind do by visiting shawmind.org or joining them on:

Twitter @Shawmind_
Facebook @ShawmindUK
Instagram @Shawmind_

Lightning Source UK Ltd.
Milton Keynes UK
UKHW041928151122
412266UK00004B/372